Deliverance Training
Manual - 201

Robert and Dixie Summers

Deliverance Training Manual - 201

Published by
Summers Ministries
Columbus, Ohio

Deliverance Training Manual - 201

Unless otherwise indicated, all scriptures used are from the New King James Version Bible

Cover Design by: CI-Media

Printed in USA

Contents

Introduction to Deliverance Training 201

The Ministry of deliverance continues to remain a core ministry of the Lord Jesus Christ. Over 2000 years ago, Jesus walked the shores of Galilee and the pristine countryside preaching the Kingdom of Heaven, and demonstrating it in part by the subsequent casting out demons of those that were oppressed. Jesus said in the gospel of Luke:

"But if I with the finger of God cast out devils, no doubt the kingdom of God is come upon you"

Prior to Calvary, Jesus gave authority over demons to those He called His apostles and disciples. Those vanguard believers were instructed to go forth and cast demons out of people and to heal those that were sick. This commission continues through to the 21st century as evidenced in Mark's Gospel:

"Go into all the world and preach the gospel to every creature. He who believes and is baptized will be saved; but he who does not believe will be condemned. And these signs will follow those who believe: In My name they will cast out demons; they will speak with new tongues; they will take up serpents; and if they drink anything deadly, it will by no means hurt them; they will lay hands on the sick, and they will recover."

The church of the living God, the body of Christ continues to have this mandate to cast out demons and heal the sick.

Demons exist today. These demon spirits have had many thousands of years to study humanity and appear to have a level of intelligence capable of deceiving even God's elect. They are strategic and are hiding in the lives of many people, cloaking themselves under the disguise of problems, dysfunction and addictions.

Each member of the Body of Christ needs to be equipped and educated in the ministry of deliverance. Unfortunately there is a shortage of quality deliverance "educators". Many believers and ministers that combat these evil forces of darkness operating in peoples lives do it the best way they know how to. Others use esoteric methods that focus more on sensationalism and dramatic operations.

In the 21st century humanity has made many advances in the areas of government, healthcare, education, business and technology among other things. However, we live in a fast paced world where the stresses of life, career, and family are sending people to the brink of suicide, sickness, disabilities and premature death. Mental health illnesses are at an all-time high.

Research shows that while many are seeking treatment, rates of those affected by mental disease have increased.

About one in ten people in the United States suffer from depression alone. Twice that number will be affected over the course of a lifetime with mood disorders like depression, bipolar disorder, dysthymia, anxiety disorders, social phobia, agoraphobia, and Obsessive-Compulsive Disorder (OCD); substance abuse; and impulse control disorder such as Attention Deficit Hyperactivity Disorder (ADHD).

And while there have been tremendous advances in clinical treatments that offer huge levels of success in helping people with mental and emotional sickness, the underlying root of the infirmity, disease and dysfunction is a spiritual one and needs to be addressed spiritually.

The purpose of this manual, Deliverance Training 201 is to provide each and every believer with the tools necessary to bring health healing and wholeness into individuals lives, as well as their own. It is our experience that many believers who receive deliverance have difficulty maintaining that deliverance or staying free from the bondage that once plagued them. This manual will provide support by delivering an understanding as to how the bound person got into the situation they're in.

As we begin the journey to understanding why we do the things we do, we will begin to heal. This journey towards deliverance and healing will give us empathy for others. As we get healed and delivered we eventually begin to live without being angry. When we're no longer judgmental and critical, it will eventually lead others to come to us for answers. The body of Christ has been sent to provide solutions to man's problems, not participate in them. One of the greatest benefits of getting yourself delivered is you can then help others. The more we help others, the more we ourselves are healed.

Deliverance 201 will also focus on how demons spirits operate, where they reside and the various methods they have for invading a person's life. Additionally, it tackles many common misconceptions of deliverance and removes the mysticism surrounding deliverance, healing and wholeness.

While this manual is comprehensive, it is not conclusive. The ministry of deliverance is vast, and new spiritual technology and revelation is constantly surfacing. Not withstanding, this manual will provide tremendous insight into the systemic problems that exist in society at-large, and the many generational dysfunctions that curse families, races and nations. The effectiveness of this manual would be greatly enhanced if studied in conjunction with our first manual, Deliverance Training 101. (Available at summersministries.com)

Deliverance is the children's bread and it is time that all believers partake of the bread.

Deliverance ministry is a wonderful ministry that has been misunderstood by some, but is needed by all. By using a balanced approach and being correctly trained, every believer can and should be equipped to set the captives free.

May God bless you richly as the eyes of your understanding are illuminated to the spiritual truth and principles of God's word surrounding balanced deliverance ministry.

Walk in your Authority,

Apostle Robert & Dixie Summers

Section One
Where Demons Reside

Where Demons Reside

When addressing the question where do demons reside, we must address this question from two distinctive viewpoints. The first question is "where demons reside when they are <u>not</u> actively demonizing the host." And the second question is, "where demons reside when they have <u>engaged</u> the host, settled in, and <u>demonized</u> the host.

What is the Host?

Before examining this, we must first clarify what is meant by the term "*host*." This term is used to define the literal person that is bound by demonic spirits. The host is the person that has created a stronghold in their soul (mind, will and emotions) and has given legal rights for demonic spirits to torment them. They are the actual, real life person that has been in bondage for perhaps decades.

It is important in deliverance ministry to consistently differentiate the host from the demons. The host is not the demon. When engaged in deliverance ministry it is critical that experienced deliverance ministers never look to eradicate or attack the host (person), but rather the demonic spirits that dwell within the host.

Unfortunately, we have witnessed numerous times where deliverance ministry has taken a turn for the worse, as enthusiastic yet unskilled believers engage the host in a manner that is uncharacteristic of the Healer. Deliverance is a ministry of compassion. It is a serving gift, designed to help hurting people. One should never attack the person in need of healing verbally or physically. People come to our churches and ministries to obtain help in their time of need. They should never leave in worse condition then when they arrived.

In many cases people are seeking answers for the problems that they have. They've been attacked over life, many since childhood from their family, spouse and others. To them, they have been victimized and traumatized. Christians need to be zealous according to knowledge and obtain the training necessary to operate with ethics, standards and Godly love.

This does not mean that the host is not responsible for the condition that they're in. In fact, it is the host that unknowingly has come into agreement with the deception and lies that these demon spirits have attacked them with.

Now, concerning the question as to "where demons reside" - Demons reside in two distinct locations: either in the **Host,** or in **Dry Places.**

The Host

In Deliverance Training Manual 101, we presented the view that demons spirits originated from the "angelic spirits" that willingly abandoned their assignment to watch over mankind. Rather, they lusted after flesh and blood, and ultimately rebelled against God's directive and perverted His creation. These once holy angels defiled themselves by lying with the daughters of man and created an offspring known as "Nephilim," or the giants.

It was after the Flood found in Genesis chapter six that God would judge these spirits and call them, "evil spirits." The evil spirits of the earth, which were born on the earth, would forever have their dwelling upon the earth. These evil spirits, birthed from the spirits of the giants, would afflict, oppress, destroy, attack, battle against and work destruction on the earth forever. They would cause trouble to mankind and bring scandal and offence. They would never cease to have an intense desire and lust to pervert their intended target – Man.

Evil spirits are demons. Their desire is to wound and ultimately destroy mankind. They have such a craving to torment man that when they are unable to do so, they themselves are tormented. This is critically important to comprehend. Demons MUST terrorize human beings. If they are not given the legal right to engage in their terroristic activities, then they themselves are in a place of torment.

The reason demons attack, torment and afflict Mankind, is because Mankind reflects the image of God. Every time a demon sees you, they see God's Glory. God's glory is the light. Demons shun the light. They love the darkness. Their goal is to extinguish the light in you by bringing in the darkness. To accomplish this goal it requires the meticulous plan of Satan. This plan is designed to keep you from excelling in life. It will attack early in life, sometimes even while the unborn child is in their mother's womb.

The effectiveness of demons is not in their ability to overpower a person, but rather in their craftiness of deceiving the targeted host. Demons utilize a cunning craft they learned from the darkness. When thinking of the darkness, one must think in terms of "that which opposes God." Darkness is misery, destruction, death, ignorance, sorrow, wickedness, and that which is kept in secret. The darkness is Satan or what can be referred to as – The Satan.

The word Satan means "adversary," - the one who opposes God and His Kingdom, both in purpose and action. Satan afflicts the soul of man. The Soul is comprised of the mind, will and emotion.

Satan has methodically developed a system whereby he uses man's own mind against himself. Deception occurs in the mind.

We see the work of Satan in the New Testament. The first instance is where Satan led Jesus into the wilderness to be tempted of the devil (Satan).

Then was Jesus led up of the Spirit into the wilderness to be tempted of the devil. And when he had fasted forty days and forty nights, he was afterward and hungered. And when the tempter came to him ….. – Matthew 4:1-3 KJV

When the adversary (Satan) came to Jesus it was not a physical Satan that spoke to him. Rather it was precisely the way that the devil talks to all to us - in our mind. Satan attacks our thought life. He fully understands that what (and how) you think, will determine who you are (or who you become). The bible says …….

For as he thinketh within himself, so is he. Proverbs 23:7 ASB

Consider also the fact that Jesus called Peter – Satan.

But he turned and said to Peter, "Get behind me, Satan! You are a hindrance to me. For you are not setting your mind on the things of God, but on the things of man." – Matthew 16:23 ESV

Jesus didn't say "Peter you're acting like Satan." No, Jesus called Peter Satan. After calling him Satan, Jesus told Peter why he called him Satan.

"Because *"you are not setting your mind on the things of God, but on the things of man."*

Anytime you do not have your mind on the things of God, His Word and Kingdom principles, you become like Satan. Some may have a hard time with this statement due to the religious indoctrination and traditional views they've subscribed to regarding who and what Satan is.

Religion and Hollywood has made Satan out to be some red-faced person with horns and a pitchfork, or God's opponent in a cosmic chess game fighting for the soul of men. Clearly the church has much to learn in regards to who, or what Satan is. Satan is real, that is without question. But much teaching in this area has lacked the use of proper biblical hermeneutics and exegesis of scripture. We will discuss Satan later in this Manual, but for now we need to address a very common misconception. Can a believer have a demon in them?

Can a Believer have a Demon in them?"

There is much confusion in regards to the ministry of deliverance that some people have sided with the idea that a born-again Christian cannot have the Spirit of God in them and at the same time have an evil spirit. Prominent leaders within the religious community exacerbate this misconception, as well as Christian Television personalities by saying, "Christians do not need deliverance because when they got saved - they got it all."

One of the first things that we hear when we talk about getting believers free from demonic bondages is, "How can demons be in a believer when the Spirit of God dwells in them?" We can address that question by asking another question. Where does the Spirit of God dwell? At the new birth, does the spirit of God indwell your spirit, soul or body? What part of you was "born-again?"

Perhaps you're thinking, "but wait, I thought I am complete In-Him." Whilst it's true that we are complete in Christ, we must understand that this is speaking specifically of our spirit man and not our body or soul.

Your spirit man was completely changed at salvation. It was totally transformed. And although your body and soul was impacted by the born-again experience, the body and soul was not made complete. The change only took place in your spirit, not your body or soul. That change needs to work it's way out into one's body and soul by the renewing of the mind. So, when it comes to being born-again, your soul wasn't the part of you that completely changed, it was only your spirit.

Consider this example. If you had a scar on your body or bills to pay prior to your conversion, did you still have that scar or those bills after conversion? Of course you did! And if you were depressed and fearful before you got save, you'll stay that way until you change the way you think by renewing your mind to what the Word of God says about you. The depression and fear did not leave you once you got saved, because the depression and fear are in your mind and emotions. Likewise, if evil spirits are present at conversion, they are probably still there after conversion.

Additionally, much of the misunderstanding has resulted from the King James Version of the Bible's translation of the Greek word *daimonizomai* as "possessed with devils." A more accurate translation is: *"to be under the power or influence of a demon or to be demonized."*

To be under the influence of something is not the same as being possessed. Possession has to do with ownership. Therefore, as believers we cannot be possessed in our spirit since Christ owns our spirit at the new birth. However, our mind, will, and emotions, have not been redeemed and are therefore subject to the influence of the enemy. The fact is that believers are being influenced and oppressed by demonic powers.

Over the years many have taught that demons possess your spirit man. This is not a statement of truth. Once your spirit man is born-again, through believing in your heart and confessing with your mouth the Lord Jesus Christ, you become a new creation.

> *..... that if you confess with your mouth the Lord Jesus and believe in your*

heart that God has raised Him from the dead, you will be saved. – Romans 10:9

Once a person gives his life to Christ he actually becomes a new creation or species. The old, that is to say, the old man where the sin nature existed, passes away and the person becomes a new living spirit.

Therefore if any man be in Christ, he is a new creature: old things are passed away; behold, all things are become new.- II Corinthians 5:17

When someone receives the Lord by believing in His name, they become spiritual sons of God.

But as many as received him, to them gave he power to become the sons of God, even to them that believe on his name: - John 1:12

Being a son of God means that the Spirit of Christ (the King) actually enters into your heart. There is an actual merging that takes place between the believer's spirit and Christ's Spirit.

And because ye are sons, God hath sent forth the Spirit of his Son into your hearts, crying, Abba, Father - Galatians 4:6

Jesus prayed to the Father that we would be one, and that we would be in both the Father and in Christ the Son.

Neither pray I for these alone, but for them also which shall believe on me through their word; That they all may be one; as thou, Father, art in me, and I in thee, that they also may be one in us ..... John 17:20-21

When we give our life to Christ the Old Man dies. We no longer live but rather Christ lives in us. Notice it did not say that Christ lives through us but in us.

I am crucified with Christ: nevertheless I live; yet not I, but Christ liveth in me: and the life which I now live in the flesh I live by the faith of the Son of God, who loved me, and gave himself for me. Galatians 2:20

Sealed

Let no corrupt communication proceed out of your mouth, but that which is good to the use of edifying, that it may minister grace unto the hearers. – Ephesians 4:29

The word sealed is the Greek word *"sphragizō"* meaning a private mark for security or preservation, to be securely sealed from Satan.

The Merriam-Webster dictionary defines it as: "a tight and perfect closure (as against the passage of something)"

You been SEALED with the Holy Spirit. Where were you sealed? In your Spirit! Demons cannot bind, oppress or possess your spirit. Jesus is in your spirit.

Even the Spirit of truth; whom the world cannot receive, because it seeth him not, neither knoweth him: but ye know him; for he dwelleth with you, and shall be in you. 20 At that day ye shall know that I am in my Father, and ye in me, and I in you. John 14:17, 20

Know ye not that ye are the temple of God, and that the Spirit of God dwelleth in you? - 1 Corinthians 3:16

The Spirit of the Living God has decided to make His abode in you. He's not going to share space with demons!

But he that is joined unto the Lord is one spirit. (not two, yours and His, ONE) What? know ye not that your body is the temple of the Holy Ghost which is in you, which ye have of God, and ye are not your own? 1 Corinthians 6:17, 19

However, some continue to argue that a believer cannot be possessed by demons. Nevertheless the fact remains that many born-again believers, including church leaders and prime-time preachers are experiencing major inhibiting struggles, dysfunctional lifestyles and perversions.

Additionally, while some say that a born-again believer cannot be demonized, our experience in deliverance and healing ministry is utterly different than that statement.

Those who believe that deliverance, healing and wholeness is not for the 21st century believer, needs to reassess their theological position and understand that demons do not possess one's spirit, but rather their Body & Soul.

Demons Bind the Soul

It is the soul (mind, will and emotions) and the body—that are the targets of demonic attack. Demons can dwell in those areas of the believer's life. When we say that a believer is demonized, we are not saying he has a demon in his spirit but rather in some part of his soul or body.

And the very God of peace sanctify you wholly; and I pray God your whole spirit and soul and body be preserved blameless unto the coming of our Lord Jesus Christ. – I Thessalonians 5:23

The Bible is very clear that mankind is a tripartite being. He is a spirit, he has a soul

16

and he lives in a body.

If you were to look in the mirror you would see your body. Your body is the physical part of you that enables you to relate and communicate in this natural-physical world. You accomplish this through what's known as the 5-senses. (Sight, Taste, Touch, Hear and Smell).

The soul originates from the spirit world and is created by God.

"Before I formed thee in the belly I knew thee..." - Jeremiah 1:5

The Bible doesn't give any clue as to when souls are created. The only thing we can ascertain for certain is that the soul is added to the new human life consisting of an egg and sperm at the moment of conception. Clearly, this does not mean that man has lived in a previous life because there is no reincarnation. Once a soul has been created, it is eternal. The soul will either live eternally with God in the Kingdom of Heaven through the process called the New Birth *(John 6:51,58 / John 3:3)* or be condemned to the Lake of Fire *(Revelation 20:11-15)*.

Your soul is the mental-emotional part of you. It is comprised of your mind, will, and emotions. Your soul was not automatically changed at the new-birth. It's subject to change, but you have the responsibility to renew your mind to experience change in your mind and emotions.

And do not be conformed to this world, but be transformed by the renewing of your mind, that you may prove what is that good and acceptable and perfect will of God. – Romans 12:2

Our minds are similar to computers in the sense that they can be programmed. And once programmed, they will continue to function as programmed until we reprogram them. Many people today, including believers, have their mind "programmed" based on the carnal way of thinking. Of course the way you think has a direct correlation to your emotions and your will, (the soul).

We must understand that there is a distinction between the "spirit" and the "soul" of man.

"For the word of God is quick, and powerful, and sharper than any two-edged sword, piercing even to the dividing asunder of soul and spirit, and of the joints and marrow, and is a discerner of the thoughts and intents of the heart" - Hebrews 4:12

Although a born-again believer cannot be demon possessed in their spirit, his or her soul and body can become the object of habitation and control by an evil spirit.

Is there scriptural support that a believer can be under the influence of a Demon?

Absolutely yes! Here are ten of examples.

1. Ananias and Sapphira were two believers in the 1st century church. Peter said "Satan had filled their heart. To "fill" means to: "occupy the whole of (or) to possess and perform the duties of."

> *"But Peter said, Ananias, why hath Satan filled thine heart to lie to the Holy Ghost, and to keep back part of the price of the land?" - Acts 5:3*

2. Simon, a Believer was under the influence of a spirit of bitterness. Clearly he was in bondage.

> *"Then Simon himself believed also: and when he was baptized, he continued with Philip, and wondered, beholding the miracles and signs which were done" - Acts 8:13*

When Simon, who was a believer, attempted to buy the miracles, Peter rebukes him saying......

> *"Repent therefore of this thy wickedness, and pray God, if perhaps the thought of thine heart may be forgiven thee. For I perceive that thou art in the gall of bitterness, and in the bond of iniquity" - Acts 8:22-23*

3. A believer can give his house/temple (his soul and body) over to the enemy.

> *"Be angry, and do not sin": do not let the sun go down on your wrath, nor give place to the devil - Ephesians 4:26-27*

4. A born-again believer can have spiritual strongholds. A stronghold is a fortified place created in the mind and emotions, which an evil spirit can embed themselves in. We will talk more on Strongholds in the section entitled "Understanding Strongholds"

> *"For the weapons of our warfare are not carnal but mighty in God for pulling down strongholds, casting down arguments and every high thing that exalts itself against the knowledge of God, bringing every thought into captivity to the obedience of Christ," - II Corinthians 10:4-5*

5. A born-again believer can be entrapped and held captive by demons.

> *"And the servant of the Lord must not strive; but be gentle unto all men, apt to*

teach, patient, In meekness instructing those that oppose themselves; if God peradventure will give them repentance to the acknowledging of the truth; And that they may recover themselves out of the snare of the devil, who are taken captive by him at his will" - II Timothy 2:24-26

6. Additionally, we see in scripture that God may turn us over to tormenting spirits if we refuse to forgive.

    "And his lord was wroth, and delivered him to the tormentors, till he should pay all that was due unto him. So likewise shall my heavenly Father do also unto you, if ye from your hearts forgive not every one his brother their trespasses" - Matthew 18:34-35

7. Furthermore, born-again believers are told to resist the devil. If there were no possibility for the devil (demons) to bind us, why would we need to resist them?

    "Submit yourselves therefore to God. Resist the devil, and he will flee from you" - James 4:7

8. Jesus called one of his own disciples "Satan."

    "But he turned, and said unto Peter, Get thee behind me, Satan:" - Matthew 16:23 (American Standard Version)

9. Paul exhorts the beloved brethren in the Philippian church to……..

    "work out your own (soul) salvation with fear and trembling ….. Philippians 2:12

Why would Paul tell born-again believers to carry out the goal, and fully complete their own salvation, when Jesus said *"it is finished"* in John 19:30?

The type of salvation spoken here by the Apostle Paul refers to deliverance and the need for the mind (part of the Soul) to be saved. The word saved is the Greek word *sōtēria;* meaning rescue, safety and deliverance.

10. The ministry of deliverance is the Kingdom rights of believers, not the unsaved.

The story of the Syrophoenician woman in *Mark 7:25-30* makes this very clear. The woman sought out Jesus so He would deliver her daughter from an unclean spirit. But Jesus told her ……..

    "Let the children be filled first, for it is not good to take the children's bread and throw it to the little dogs."– Mark 7:27

The phrase *"the children's bread"* refers to deliverance. Deliverance belongs to Kingdom citizens not those outside the Kingdom (*Revelation 22:15*) Those outside the gates of the Kingdom, may receive a miracle from God, based on His mercy, but it's clear from scripture that deliverance is meant for the born-again believer.

Misconception: Demons gain access through your Spirit

While this may be true for an unbeliever, it is not true for a born-again believer. The Soul realm (mind, will and emotions) is the main gate by which demons are granted access into one's life.

As believers we know that the life we live is by faith in the Son of God and is based solely on the grace of God. There is nothing that can defile our spirit-man. We have been made new and have been forever sealed by the Holy Spirit. However, WE are responsible for renewing our minds. When we do not guard the way we think about others, our environment, or ourselves we open the door for the enemy to bring accusations against us.

2 Corinthians 10:4-5 provides insight into this:

"For the weapons of our warfare are not carnal, but mighty through God to the pulling down of strong holds; Casting down imaginations, and every high thing that exalteth itself against the knowledge of God, and bringing into captivity every thought to the obedience of Christ;"

When we do not engage in warfare the enemy can devour our lives. Warfare occurs in the battlefield of the mind. Our spiritual weapons were designed for the express purpose of taking thoughts captive and making them obedient to the image of who we are in Christ. If we have not been equipped properly, or we are negligent in this area, then that which is in opposition to the knowledge of God, (i.e. darkness) can become a stronghold.

A stronghold is a fortified and safe place that demons can dwell in. Once a stronghold is created in the mind, bondage occurs. This bondage will affect other areas, specifically the emotions and physical parts of the body. We will explore the area of "Strongholds" deeper in the section entitled "Understanding Strongholds."

Dry Places

Now let's explore where demons reside when they're not in a host. Certainly, there has been much discussion regarding this question over the years. Visit any bookshelf in a Christian bookstore and you'll find a vast array of publications suggesting that demons make their abode in hell. Typically they will give pictures of the demons not only living there themselves but thriving and ultimately beating up on and punishing those souls that have been sentenced to hell. Further imagery gives colorful pictures of demons being assigned by Satan to attack nations, churches, government, finances and people. While this notion may retail well and present itself nicely in cartoons or theatrical Hollywood performances, it is simply not scriptural truth.

To purge ourselves of any religious indoctrination in this area, we should objectively start by asking the sincere question, "Where do demons and evil spirit reside when they are not in a host?" To answer this question, we must look to gather a better understanding of the Kingdom of Darkness, specifically Satan and Demons.

Satan

As one gravitates towards the truth, one must be able to differentiate between evil spirits. Specifically, Satan, demons and his fallen angels. We understand that Satan is an evil spirit, and then of course Satan has angels. These angels have been commonly referred to as fallen Angels. The authors choose to use the term "Satan's angels" as it is more biblically sound then the term fallen Angels. We can clearly see in scripture that there is a place reserved for both Satan and his angels.

Then shall he say also unto them on the left hand, Depart from me, ye cursed, into everlasting fire, prepared for the devil and his angels: Matt 25:41

When we look at the Scriptures through the lens of fulfilled eschatology, rather than theoretical views that insert personal bias into the text, we will have a clearer understanding of the new covenant, what Christ accomplished at Calvary, the ascension and Parousia. Proper comprehension of the word of God clearly reflects that Satan and his angels have been completely defeated. This defeat does not suggest that Satan and his angels no longer exists, but rather tell us where they exist.

In the old covenant the devil and his angels did have a level of authority over mankind. We know this to be true because in Luke's gospel we see Jesus did not dispute what the devil said in relation to the authority that he had, or that he could give that authority to whomsoever he willed.

And the devil said unto him, All this power will I give thee, and the glory of them: for that is delivered unto me; and to whomsoever I will I give it. Luke 4:6

Additionally, in the books of Job and Daniel, we understand Satan had the liberty to roam about and seek out those he would afflict.

Now there was a day when the sons of God came to present themselves before the Lord, and Satan came also among them. And the Lord said unto Satan, Whence comest thou? Then Satan answered the Lord, and said, From going to and fro in the earth, and from walking up and down in it. Job 1:6-7

Then said he unto me, Fear not, Daniel: for from the first day that thou didst set thine heart to understand, and to chasten thyself before thy God, thy words were heard, and I am come for thy words. But the prince of the kingdom of Persia withstood me one and twenty days: but, lo, Michael, one of the chief princes, came to help me; and I remained there with the kings of Persia - Daniel 10:12-13

However, while Satan <u>had</u> limited authority over the earth and mankind, once Christ came and defeated the enemy, all the rule, power and dominion was secured by Christ.

And the seventh angel sounded; and there were great voices in heaven, saying, The kingdoms of this world are become the kingdoms of our Lord, and of his Christ; and he shall reign for ever and ever. Rev 11:15

Now is the judgment of this world: now shall the prince of this world be cast out. John 12:31

These Scriptures are not future events yet to occur. Rather they are events that took place in the 1st century. The word "now" can never speak of an event some 2000 years (or more) removed from the audience to whom it spoken to.

Therefore, with the death, burial, resurrection, ascension and Parousia of the Lord in the 1st century, it is evident and without exception, that Satan and his angels have been bound forever.

And I saw an angel come down from heaven, having the key of the bottomless pit and a great chain in his hand. And he laid hold on the dragon, that old serpent, which is the Devil, and Satan, and bound him a thousand years, And cast him into the bottomless pit, and shut him up, and set a seal upon him ……. - Rev20 1:3(a)

And the devil that deceived them was cast into the lake of fire and brimstone, where the beast and the false prophet are, and shall be tormented day and night for ever and ever - Rev 20:10

For if God spared not the angels that sinned, but cast them down to hell, and delivered them into chains of darkness, to be reserved unto judgment - II Peter 2:4

And the angels which kept not their first estate, but left their own habitation, he hath reserved in everlasting chains under darkness unto the judgment of the great day - Jude 1:6

And I heard a loud voice saying in heaven, Now is come salvation, and strength, and the kingdom of our God, and the power of his Christ: for the accuser of our brethren is cast down, which accused them before our God day and night - Rev 12:10

The accuser of the brethren is cast down and therefore no longer is able to come before God and accuse us to Him.

Scripture reveals that Satan and his angels were doomed for a place of judgment. That place of judgment is called the 'lake of fire.' The lake of fire is prophetic symbolism that represents God's judgment, specifically on and against Satan. It is also referred to the 'abyss' or the 'bottomless pit'. This is a place of eternal darkness. It is the _underworld_.

Hell from _beneath_ is moved for thee to meet thee at thy coming .... - Isaiah 14:9
(a)

That at the name of Jesus every knee should bow, of things in heaven, and things in earth, and things under the earth - Phil 2:10

The underworld is the place in the unseen realm that is reserved for Satan and his angels. They are there now. As such, they have absolutely no authority over a believer. Again, this does not mean that Satan and his angels do not exist, but rather, that they exist in a place of judgment to be tormented day and night forever.

Understanding where Satan resides requires a proper, hermeneutically sound eschatological view. If one's view of the "end of the age" is flawed, then perhaps - "Satan is alive and well on Planet Earth," (Hal Lindsey 1970 Zondervan).

Jesus defeated the Devil. So, where did Satan go when Jesus defeated him? The bible says:

And the devil that deceived them was cast into the lake of fire and brimstone, where the beast and the false prophet are, and shall be tormented day and night forever and ever. Rev 20:10

Satan in the Lake of Fire

Satan is in the lake of fire – now! The lake of fire is prophetic typology and symbolism of Judgment. It is a place of eternal torment for Satan. The bible says, Satan and his demonic Kingdom are perpetually tormented "day and night – forever." This means there is no end for Satan but rather he is condemned to the "Pit" and "Abyss." Satan now resides in the unseen realm in the place of darkness.

Jesus removed Satan from his seat of authority over 2,000 years ago. Christ himself stated, *"It is finished."* The plan of redemption and the complete work of Christ are past tense. In Luke chapter 10, it records at time when Jesus sent 70 of His followers out to preach and demonstrate the Kingdom. Upon returning, they give a report of what happened.

And the seventy returned again with joy, saying, Lord, even the devils are subject unto us through thy name. And he said unto them, I beheld Satan as lightning fall from heaven. Behold, I give unto you power to tread on serpents and scorpions, and over all the power of the enemy: and nothing shall by any means hurt you. – Luke 10:17-19

Jesus witnessed Satan *"fall from heaven as lighting"* as the seventy returned from casting out demons and setting the captives free. This is apocalyptic language used to indicate Satan being removed from his seat of authority he once had. In the 1st century, the disciples witnessed the demise of Satan's Kingdom.

And the God of peace shall bruise Satan under your feet shortly. – Romans 16:20

For this purpose the Son of God was manifested, that he might destroy the works of the devil. – I John 3:8

Jesus was successful in destroying the occupation of the devil. There is no record in the bible that indicates that Satan ever recovered from this defeat and resumed any power. Rather, the King of Kings and Lord of Lords stripped him of all authority, relocated him from being the "God of this World' to his final place of torment, the Lake of Fire.

What about Demons?

Demons have been spiritually bound as well. However, just like Satan, they exist as well. They are the powers of the dark world that we wrestle against.

*For our struggle is not against flesh and blood, but against the rulers, against the authorities, against **the powers of this dark world** and against the spiritual forces of evil in the heavenly realms Eph 6:12 NIV*

Demons are not to be confused with Satan or his angels. For additional teaching on this topic, please refer to our **Deliverance Training Manual - 101**.

Demons have been judged and bound; yet they do retain a purpose in the dark underworld, and that is to torment mankind.

Much information can be found in the book of I Enoch regarding demons. The book of I Enoch is a non-canonical book and consequently should be read with considerable cynicism. However it does provide much insight pertaining to these demon spirits. Worthy to note is the fact that Jude himself references the writings of Enoch.

And He answered and said to me, and I heard His voice: 'Fear not, Enoch, thou righteous 2 man and scribe of righteousness: approach hither and hear my voice. And go, say to the Watchers of heaven, who have sent thee to intercede for them:

"You should intercede" for men, and not men 3 for you: Wherefore have ye left the high, holy, and eternal heaven, and lain with women, and defiled yourselves with the daughters of men and taken to yourselves wives, and done like the children 4 of earth, and begotten giants (as your) sons? And though ye were holy, spiritual, living the eternal life, you have defiled yourselves with the blood of women, and have begotten (children) with the blood of flesh, and, as the children of men, have lusted after flesh and blood as those also do who die 5 and perish. Therefore have I given them wives also that they might impregnate them, and beget 6 children by them, that thus nothing might be wanting to them on earth. But you were formerly 7 spiritual, living the eternal life, and immortal for all generations of the world. And therefore I have not appointed wives for you; for as for the spiritual ones of the heaven, in heaven is their dwelling. 8 And now, the giants, who are produced from the spirits and flesh, shall be called evil spirits upon 9 the earth, and on the earth shall be their dwelling. Evil spirits have proceeded from their bodies; because they are born from men and from the holy Watchers is their beginning and primal origin; 10 they shall be evil spirits on earth, and evil spirits shall they be called. [As for the spirits of heaven, in heaven shall be their dwelling, but as for the spirits of the earth which were born upon the earth, on the earth shall be their dwelling.] And the spirits of the giants afflict, oppress, destroy, attack, do battle, and work destruction on the earth, and cause trouble: they take no food, but nevertheless 12 hunger and thirst, and cause offences. And these spirits shall rise up against the children of men and against the women, because they have proceeded from them." - I Enoch 15: 1-12

Enoch operated at an elevated spiritual level. He was able to see in the unseen realm as he "walked by faith not by sight (seen realm). It appears that Enoch received revelation and spiritual insight pertaining to demonic spirits.

Notice that this offspring that was produced by spirits and flesh:

1. Shall be called evil spirits on the Earth
2. Earth shall be there dwelling
3. They will afflict, oppress, destroy, attack, cause trouble and offences
4. Opposes mankind

These are certainly the characteristics of demons spirits.

However, demons do not walk the earth *per se*. Demons are not physical beings but rather spiritual beings. When Jesus walked this earth in the 1st century demons were fearful of him. In one case, they were so fearful of being tormented "before their time".

And, behold, they cried out, saying, What have we to do with thee, Jesus, thou Son of God? art thou come hither to torment us before the time? - Matt 8:29

Demons were so fearful of being tormented that they asked to go into a heard of swine. This time of tormenting would occur at the Eschatological (*end of the old covenant age*) binding of Satan and his kingdom by Jesus. Satan's kingdom included his angels (that secured the 2nd heaven) as well as demons that roamed the earth.

Demon's desire and lust to be in a Soul of man. If they can't reside in a human being, they will settle for an animal. However they have no desire nor can reside in inanimate objects. Many people today believe that demon's possess or are in artifacts, paintings, statues and clothing. This is false teaching that has zero credibility or scriptural basis.

Demons do gathering around the occult, pagan rituals and items that are idolized by people, but they are not in the object. This improper teaching has lead many to not touch or be in the vicinity of evil objects for fear of demons "transferring" or "hopping" onto a person. This mindset is exacerbated by the numerous movies projecting demons on the big screen as having this ability. While it may be entertaining to some, it is simply not truthful.

Jesus gives us further insight as to what happens when a demon spirit is extracted from a person.

When the unclean spirit is gone out of a man, he walketh through dry places, seeking rest …….. - Luke 11:24

Jesus said that demons walk through dry places in an attempt to obtain rest. Demons can never obtain rest because their hunger is that of mankind. I Enoch stated that demons would always *hunger and thirst and look to cause offense* to mankind.

This dry place is not speaking of a physical place but rather a spiritual habitation. The "dry place" is not the desert, but rather the unseen realm where demons cannot express themselves and oppress mankind.

The word "dry" is the Greek word *"anydros"* meaning waterless or without water. This indicates that the "dry place" is a place where there is no life. Water refreshes, cools and irrigates. It is essential for human beings physical survival. Water represents man. On average, an adult human body is comprised of 65% water.

When a demon is cast out or not in a host, they are lifeless and ineffective. They are in a place of torment called the abyss. The Abyss is the unseen realm and a place of judgment. Demons are very fearful of being in the dry place of torment (i.e. the Abyss) and do not want to have any part with it.

Jesus asked him, saying, "What is your name?" And he said, "Legion," because many demons had entered him. And they begged Him that He would not command them to go out into the abyss. – Luke 8:30-31

Remember the "Abyss" is a spiritual (unseen) place representing continual judgment and torment. When demons are cast out of a person they are tormented. They know that when they are cast out of a person or do not have "legal access" to enter in, they cannot function in the earth for they are in "dry places."

Demons must stay in the "dry place" and experience torment. They do not have the authority or the power (ability) to free themselves from this judgment. They can only function in the earth realm when a person (mankind – human being) opens the door and invites them in.

Demons need access points. There must be a door. Demons do not create the doors. People create doors. There is no such thing as a demon having "illegal" access. Demons use the following access points:

- Thoughts
- Emotions
- Corresponding Actions

Those that walk in the flesh open the door to demons. Demons are given legal access when one engages in a sinful lifestyle, is disobedient to God's word, bitter, unforgiving, emotionally and/or mentally agrees with the darkness.

Conclusion

Demons desire to express themselves through a human body. A demon is not effective unless he has a human body. Because demons do not possess physical bodies of their own, demons seek to inhabit or use the bodies of humans or animals. When demons are not in a host, they are in a "dry and uninhabited" placed of torment.

Section Notes:

Section Two
Understanding Strongholds

Understanding Strongholds

The word "stronghold" can mean *a well-fortified city or fortress*. A stronghold is a central place of _agreed-upon_ thoughts and views. It is the *driving force* behind one's attitudes, behaviors and actions. A demonic stronghold is deception that's taken hold in a person's mind. It's an incorrect thinking pattern based on a believed lie. A stronghold is also an emotional safe haven that protects you from *perceived harm*.

Strongholds can be good or evil. For instance, someone who fears rejection may take relief or comfort in imaginative mindsets of revenge or retaliation towards those who have rejected him or her. This is classified as an "evil or demonic stronghold."

An example of a good or positive stronghold would be if someone's faith in Christ or Salvation were challenged. Perhaps they were told that they're going to hell when they die. A good stronghold would render the person completely unaffected by this comment. There's nothing anyone could say that would get him or her to change the way they think about their security in salvation.

Wrong teaching on Strongholds

Before moving forward in understanding spiritual strongholds, we must learn what they are not.

Many people today, teach that stronghold's are in the atmosphere, hemisphere, and stratosphere, and that they are encamped over cities all across the world. Certainly it's true; some stronghold's can be territorial strongholds. There are demonic powers, principalities, and rulers that establish strongholds on the earth. Many of these are manifested through political parties, establishments, religions, cultures, sectors and races. However, what is important to understand is that they are established through a particular way of thinking of the indigenous population within the region.

The resulting bondage may be seen in areas such as poor economic growth, poverty, depression, fear, pride or corruption.

Unfortunately today, many people have taken what Paul was talking about regarding spiritual warfare and strongholds out of context. They have developed esoteric teachings that have severely hindered individuals from getting free. Some have even gone as far as stating that there are demons hovering around and over cities, somehow embedded in the atmosphere.

This teaching creates a mindset that Satan and his demonic henchmen somehow have sovereign power to rule over territories, regions and nations. Some will even say that these demonic strongholds have the ability to block the prayers of the righteous from getting through to God. Much of this incorrect teaching comes from those that extrapolate inaccurately from the Book of Daniel. Here we see the Angel of the Lord saying to Daniel ....

"Do not fear, Daniel, for from the first day that you set your heart to understand, and to humble yourself before your God, your words were heard; and I have come because of your words. But the prince of the kingdom of Persia withstood me twenty-one days; and behold, Michael, one of the chief princes, came to help me, for I had been left alone there with the kings of Persia. – Daniel 10:12-13

Many people perceive that the strongholds they need to pull down are in the atmosphere surrounding the earth. This is far from the truth because you have to take what Paul was saying in context. To understand in context, you need to ask and answer some questions from Paul's second letter to the Corinthian church:

(For the weapons of our warfare are not carnal, but mighty through God to the pulling down of strong holds;) Casting down imaginations, and every high thing that exalteth itself against the knowledge of God, and bringing into captivity every thought to the obedience of Christ; - II Corinthians 10:4-5 (KJV)

Questions:

1. Where is your imagination exercised?
2. Where do things exalt itself against the knowledge of God?
3. Where are your thoughts processed?

All of these things occur in you Soul (mind, will and emotions). Your imaginations are exercised in your mind; your knowledge of God is developed and challenged in and through your intellect, while your thoughts are processed in your mind.

It's not only ridiculous but also irresponsible to teach that the strongholds Paul is talking about is somehow in the "gases surrounding the earth."

Nevertheless, what is commonly (but inaccurately) taught from this scripture is that there are demonic forces in the atmosphere that are prohibiting the move of God over regions. They define these as "strongholds."

Of course to eliminate those forces, religious personnel call for Christians to release warfare-type prayers to contend with the "spiritual strongholds" in the heavenlies. Further, bands of intercessors must engage in "pulling down" these atmospheric strongholds and the region must be saturated with dynamic praise and worship music, complete with banners and dancers. Finally, if that doesn't work, the saints must fast, prophesy, declare and decree that the enemy leave that region. Once this is done, then apparently all of the crime, poverty and corruption in the area are mystically eradicated. Here's the question; "How's that been working?"

After the countless hours of prayer, the millions of dollars spent on church revivals, conference and gatherings and the prophetic "pulling down of strongholds in the region, nothing measurable has changed. Our cities continue to deteriorate, social and economic chaos increases and families are more dysfunctional than ever.

Certainly, the saints need to be praying, prophesying, fasting, worshipping and gathering together. And yes, there are demonic forces at work in the air that terrorize our cities, nations and races. But how we deal with them is not by these non-scriptural activities, but rather by renewing the minds and changing the hearts of the people that occupy those territories. You can't control demonic forces in the heavenlies by your prayers and therefore indirectly control the people from engaging in ungodly behaviors, simply because you're saying you're "pulling down strongholds." Why is that?

Because, this is not the type of confrontation the Apostle Paul is talking about.

What is a "Stronghold?"

In the Apostle Paul's second letter to the Corinthian church he gives us some understanding as to what a stronghold is.

For though we walk in the flesh, we do not war according to the flesh. For the weapons of our warfare are not carnal but mighty in God for pulling down strongholds, casting down arguments and every high thing that exalts itself against the knowledge of God, bringing every thought into captivity to the obedience of Christ, - II Corinthians 10:3-5

Some keys words derived from the scriptural text about is:

- Imagination
- Thoughts
- Pull down
- Cast down
- Captivity

Rather, Paul is discussing *strongholds* as *mindsets* that open the door to bondage (enslavement). The strongholds Paul is talking about are:

- Erroneous beliefs, and teachings that lead to "acts of disobedience"
- Religious lies and deceptions the enemy uses to enslave us to his ways of thinking, attitudes, and actions.
- Arguments that come against a true understanding (the knowledge) of God – The Word of God

For though we walk in the flesh, we do not war after the flesh: (For the weapons of our warfare are not carnal, but mighty through God to the pulling down of strong holds;) Casting down imaginations, and every high thing that exalteth itself against the knowledge of God, and bringing into captivity every thought to the obedience of Christ; And having in a readiness to revenge all disobedience, when your obedience is fulfilled. - II Corinthians 10:3-6

In Paul's day, strongholds in the mind possibly included keeping certain man-made traditions, or following particular religious rules, laws, and regulations. These were attempts to please God through "works" rather than accepting Christ finished work at Calvary and salvation by grace, through faith. Clearly there were some in the Corinthian church who were promoting legalism over grace, promiscuity over self-discipline and perversion over holiness.

Notice in context, Paul is talking about pulling down strongholds; he also tells us how to do it.

- Casting down imaginations
- Bringing thoughts into captivity

Meaning of terminology used in II Corinthians 10:3-6

- Casting down – *"kathairesis"* - To destroy something by force, to detach.
- Imaginations – *"logismos"* - to reason, to form a mental image of something.
- Captive (captivity) – *"aichmalōtizō";* to be lead away, taken prisoner,
- Thoughts – *"noēma"* - a mental perception or disposition.
- High thing – *"hypsōma"* - demonic activities and ideas (built high in the mind, will and emotions), a wall, elevated structure.

The Greek word used to describe "imaginations" is "Logismos." It is portrayed here as a reasoning that is hostile to Christ and His Word. In the Living Bible it is translated by the phrase *"every proud argument against God."* The "high things" include anything that opposes or blocks the true knowledge about God, Christ, the Holy Spirit and His Creation as revealed in the Word of God.

Clearly, Paul is telling us that mental images that go against God's word, regardless of how strong they are, need to be destroyed. Further, we must come out of agreement with the lies of the enemy that has been released against our life through words by our self and others. In short, we are to take our thinking captive to the obedience of the Word of God, to the point where we believe the Word, we say the Word, and we do the Word. When we fill our mind with the Word, it becomes a slave that is captive to the truth. Initially we accomplish this by breaking our agreement with the lies and arguments against God and who we are In-Him.

It is critically important to comprehend that it is the mind that is the amphitheater in which thoughts and reasoning contrary to God's Word are to be captured and submitted to the Word of God. Paul was saying that the reason we have spiritual weapons (i.e. *Eph 6:10*) is for the explicit purpose of taking thoughts captive and making them obedient to Christ.

In the 21st century, two of the most common and devastating strongholds are:

- **An incorrect perception of God**
- **An incorrect perception of Self**

Incorrect Perception of God

When one has an *incorrect perception of God* it creates a stronghold that significantly hinders them from achieving their genuine purpose in life. Rather than seeing God as a loving, kind, compassionate, forgiving and merciful God, they see Him as a punishing, un-loving and condemning God.

Many times those that have an inaccurate view of God express anger towards God and blame Him for the trauma and pain they have experienced in life, specifically in their early childhood. Additionally, they have an irrational and corrupt fear of Him, which prevents them from drawing close to Him.

When one does not have a perception that God is a loving and forgiving God, they will feel unwanted, and unloved by Him. They may have a difficult time trusting Him and typically end up being bound by a spirit of pride, rebellion and fear. They may wonder if He will really come through for them in a time of need. Often this will lead to control, manipulation, domination and intimidation operating in the person as they feel that they must control everything. This is a precursor to developing a Narcissistic Personality Disorder.

Incorrect Perception of Self

When a person has an *incorrect perception of self*, it can create a stronghold that seriously prohibits them from becoming successful and excelling in life. Rather than identifying themselves the way God identifies them, they suffer from an identity disorder strengthened by a demonic stronghold. This stronghold has them believing the lies of the enemy, rather than the Word of God.

The enemy lies and wants to get us to think our identity is associated with the things we struggle with, or what someone else says about us. When a person has a inward view that's inconsistent with the Word of God, and diametrically opposes how God views us, this stronghold can lead to a dysfunctional life, perverted relationships and addictions of the flesh. This ancient strategy of the enemy is for us to believe that we actually 'are' how we feel or behave, rather than what the Word of God says about us.

"Never let a past circumstance or current events steal your true identity. "

A person that has an incorrect perception of self is prone to enabling the following strongholds to develop in their life.

- Low self-Esteem
- Poor self-image
- Guilt
- Shame
- Worthlessness
- Depression
- Condemnation
- Self-Accusation

A **Low self-esteem** or a poor self-image is where a person is constantly looking down upon himself or herself. This type of stronghold affects the emotional arena as the person is always seeing himself or herself as insignificant or a failure.

A **guilty conscience** is when a person doesn't perceive them self as a new creation in Christ, who's sins have been forgiven, and is now a new creation In Him *(II Cor 5:17)*

Guilt is where somebody focus's in on their failure.

Shame is when a person has a painful feeling of humiliation or distress caused by the consciousness of wrong thoughts and behaviors. Shame is where a person looks at himself or herself as the failure. Many people experience chronic shame. Chronic shame is when a person sees himself or herself as incomplete and not as a whole person. They view themselves as flawed, inferior due to their performance or actions.

Worthlessness comes from measuring one's position as being bad against many other standards. Feelings of worthlessness are entirely subjective. They are all in the mind. They have no basis in reality. This develops due to believing the lies of the enemy rather than the intrinsic value that is placed in them by God. If a person feels worthless, they will be unable to walk confidently and do the work that God has for them to do.

Depression is when a person feels sad or hopeless. They typically lack focus in life, feel sad and lack interest in accomplishing things in life. Many that experience depression do so due to the absence of God in their life. They may feel that they been abandoned by God or those that should love and support them. Some signs of depression may be changes in appetite, weight loss or gain unrelated to dieting, trouble sleeping or perhaps sleeping too much. Many experience loss of energy or increased fatigue, or have difficulty concentrating and making decisions. Depression is tied to shame and guilt and can trigger thoughts of death or suicide.

Condemnation stems from poor self-image, guilt, childhood labels, shame, critical parenting and other sources. Condemnation will have a person saying things like; "it's all my fault and God will never forgive me for what I did." Many that have a stronghold of condemnation can't forgive themselves and feel as though they deserve the pain and abuse that they've gone through, or are going through.

Self-Accusation is the act of criticizing oneself for something one has done or the feeling that they are perpetually blamable for bad decisions made. It is tied to the rejection they experienced early in life, specifically from their immediate family and has them look to tear down his/her own self-worth. It is mostly encountered when depression is agitated. Their focus is on "self." It is an internal view that has them thinking everything is their fault and that the reason people abuse them is because they deserve it.

Most of this can lead to demons of rejection, pride and rebellion manifesting in one's life.

Toxic Thinking

Again, a demonic stronghold is a defective way of thinking based on lies, deception and emotional stimulus. Strongholds in our mind are an assortment of ideas that are not in alignment with the Word of God, or His plans and purpose for your life. A stronghold is a toxic-thinking pattern that has molded itself into our way of thinking. The _way_ you think is called a philosophy. Strongholds affect our emotions, our will and how we respond to various situations in life (actions). A stronghold is a thought pattern that affects your view of the world, yourself and others.

A Stronghold exists when we are unable to accept the truth found in God's Word, or we cannot consistently follow them. They are established when we open doors to Satan through demonic (negative) belief systems (thoughts). The unfortunate truth is that many have cooperated with the enemy and have erected fortified walls in their soul. This wall is what is called a stronghold. It was built over time, brick by brick as we cooperated with the lies of Satan, whether consciously or unconsciously.

Strongholds exist in the mind. Strongholds represent a secured place that _you create_ by agreeing with life circumstances, events or what was (or is) said about you. They are developed through your _belief system_ of who you are and what the world around you is.

The reason a stronghold is developed is to protect us from further hurt and emotional trauma. However, a stronghold is counter-productive as it presents a false narrative of who you really are, based on God's word.

Once a Stronghold develops it becomes an area where a particular strongman has the _ability_ or power to control. It is the place where a strongman has _legal authority_ to operate.

As a Stronghold goes through its vicious cycles, eventually we become bound so tightly that it is almost impossible to break free from its hold. When we cannot break free from the **STRONGHOLD**, the **STRONGMAN** has taken residence. Once the strongman occupies the stronghold, he will not leave until a greater power comes.

Strongholds create an activity of thought or a unique style of thinking called a philosophy. It is the way you think or approach a matter. If the philosophy is carnal then the stronghold is devilish, worldly and sensual. Over time, strongholds become fortified through continuous fleshly (carnal) thoughts. Rather than pulling down imaginations and taking thoughts captive, many have agreed to what Satan says about them.

Satan is the father of lies. Anything thought or imagination that is in contradiction of the Word of God, specifically what the Word (God) says about His creation (us) is a lie.

He (Satan) was a murderer from the beginning, and does not stand in the truth, because there is no truth in him. When he speaks a lie, he speaks from his own resources, for he is a liar and the father of it – John 8:44

Thoughts and Imaginations build Strongholds

When you believe the lies of the enemy, you build a habitation called a Stronghold. A stronghold can be considered a house built in your soul. Thoughts and imaginations build the house for the strongman and his demons to reside in. Demons are attracted to thoughts. Habitual negative thoughts are "welcome signs" to demons. When we continually think on negative thoughts about our self we are essentially decorating the house that makes it conducive for demons to reside.

Once the house is decorated it becomes attractive to 'like kind' qualities demons. The Bible calls these the 'goods.'

But if I cast out devils by the Spirit of God, then the kingdom of God is come unto you. Or else how can one enter into a strong man's house, and spoil his goods, except he first bind the strong man? and then he will spoil his house – Matt 12:24-29 KJV

Your thoughts are what give permission to the strong man to enter in. He's attracted to how you decorate your mind with thoughts. This is why the Bible says…

For as he thinketh in his heart, so is he …. Proverbs 23:7 (a)

The goods are demons that were invited in by wrong thought patterns and emotional trauma that is focused on. When you do not take control over how you think, and then believe the lies of the enemy, it is a way of saying that you are in agreement to those lies. Demons are attracted to the lies of their father Satan.

When someone manifests in demonic characteristics such as rejection or rebellion it is the goods manifesting. To manifest means to come to the open or be revealed. When the goods (demons) manifest you are telling everyone where your thoughts are and how you think about yourself and the world around you.

Manifestations can be fear, hatred, perversion, lust, gossip, lying etc.

The more you "manifest" the more comfortable you're making it for the inevitable STRONGMAN to move in and bind you.

Remember, Satan wants you to believe things like: you're depressed, worthless, stupid, a failure and so on. He uses the rejection you've experienced from your family, and the abuse or trauma that occurred earlier in life. Pain, abuse and trauma are all real but you are not the pain – you are not the trauma. The strategy of the enemy is to get you to believe that you are that situation, event or issue.
Since strongholds are built upon lies that we have been fed (and believed), the way we tear down strongholds is by eating on the truth of God's Word.

You must expose the lies that are lodged in your mind by first identifying them. You must renounce your agreement with the darkness. Repenting of any sinful action and diligently renewing your mind on a daily basis is how we close the door to the enemy and root out any demonic strongholds.

Indications of Demonic Stronghold's

Below are **some indications of potential Demonic Strongholds**

Chronic perverted dreams	Inferiority complex	Emotionally withdrawn
Easily or constantly offended	Endlessly Exaggerating	Hyper -Sensitive
Difficulty giving or receiving love	Constantly seeking approval	Overprotective and possessive
Extremely permissive and tolerant	Unwarranted perfectionism	Extremely impulsive and irresponsible
Domineering & controlling	Self-centered, selfish	Defensive
Workaholic	Lazy, unconcerned or lethargic	Shifting blame

Recurring memories of a past hurt(s)	Chronic memory loss, inaccurate memories or inability to remember childhood	Focused on faults of self and others
Chronic Pessimism	Fascinated with cleanliness	Extreme introversion
Easily controlled by people	Struggle with addictions. (Alcohol, drugs, food, sex)	Overwhelming feelings of guilt
Easily influenced	Stubborn & Prideful	Chronic masturbator
Difficulty forgiving people	Bitter & retaliatory	Easily critical of others
Unhealthily independent	Cold & callous	Fearful, suspicious and distrustful
Inability to read or complete a task	Difficultly giving and receiving gifts	Avoid relationships
Procrastination	Fabricates & lies constantly	Inability or fear of handling money (responsibility)
Fear of Marriage	Multiple divorces	Numerous children out of wedlock
Lustful & promiscuous	Fascination with clergy	Generational Poverty

Conclusion

Through your belief system of who you are and what the world around you is – is how you create strongholds. A stronghold in the mind is a spiritual fortress made of wrong thoughts, a fortified dwelling place where demonic forces can hide and operate in power against you. The thoughts and imaginations that make up the stronghold are based on lies and deception of the enemy that challenges the truth of what God has said about you. Wrong ideas about God are not automatically eliminated when you are born again, but must be contended with by casting them down and taking them captive.

Section Notes:

40

Section Three
Understanding the Strongman

Understanding the Strongman

The strong man is the demonic personality in charge and responsible for a maintaining the stronghold. It is the demonic entity embedded within septic thoughts and imaginations within the hosts Soul.

The strongman is that which exalt himself against the knowledge and plans of God.

Now when the Pharisees heard it they said, "This fellow does not cast out demons except by Beelzebub, the ruler of the demons."But Jesus knew their thoughts, and said to them: "Every kingdom divided against itself is brought to desolation, and every city or house divided against itself will not stand. If Satan casts out Satan, he is divided against himself. How then will his kingdom stand? And if I cast out demons by Beelzebub, by whom do your sons cast them out? Therefore they shall be your judges. But if I cast out demons by the Spirit of God, surely the kingdom of God has come upon you. Or how can one enter a strong man's house and plunder his goods, unless he first binds the strong man? And then he will plunder his house. – Matthew 12:24-29

The strongman is the ruling principality (evil spirit) that controls your life (soul). When the strongman gains legal access he rules over your soul and you (the host) submits to him. This is called "bondage."

The strongman rarely operates alone. Typically he will have other evil spirits (demons) operating under his authority and domain. Because the strongman is the ruling spirit, he will employ other demons spirits that work with him.

For example: Bitterness is a Strongman or ruling spirit. But under his authority are resentment, unforgiveness, hatred, anger, retaliation, wrath, rage, violence and murder. Many times these are referred to as the 'lesser demons.'

The strongman gains legal access. He is an armed robber but he does not "break in." It's as if he (the strongman) was casing the neighborhood and noticed the decorations of your house (soul). They looked attractive to him. A soul that is dark, dysfunctional, in disarray, despair, and negative and chaotic is highly attractive for strongmen and demons.

Each strongman manifests itself through the addition of other demons employed and assigned by him, to work chaos in your life. The strength of the strongman can be found in his ability to go undetected. Strongmen are highly intelligent commanders of the Kingdom of Darkness. They are strategic and understand how to develop and execute a battle plan that enables them to occupy foreign territory.

Once a strongman takes control he conceals himself by bringing in lesser demons. These lesser demons are numerous and faithfully comply with the demands of the ruling principality. We must recognize that the strong man is "fully armed." He does not work alone. His armour is tightly pieced together as he brings in demon spirits to further solidify the bondage of the host.

Demon spirits work in groups and rarely work alone. Each group of demons has a leader called the strongman. The strongman is the ruling demon over a group of demons. The strongman is the dominant demon and considers the persons mind, will and emotions (and body) to be his own (house). Demons are linked together similar to the links in a chain. The chain has many levels or rankings. This chain creates a highly organized network of demonic spirits that binds a person, leaving them defeated, all at the direction of a ruling principality called – The Strongman.

Once the strongman has moved into the fortified house (called a stronghold) he refers to it as "his house."

*I will return unto **my house** whence I came out …… Luke 11:24*

The term "my house" describes possession. You don't have to own something to possess it. The strongman, with his network of demons do not own your soul, they simply have taken control over it. For example, you can have control over the automobile that you drive daily to work, but not own it. You're in possession of it but you don't own it. That's precisely how it works with the strongman.

There are times in deliverance ministry where people do not get completely set free. Many in deliverance ministry lack the training in understanding how the Kingdom of Darkness operates and the process of "sweeping" one's house (soul) clean of demonic principalities and strongholds. The average minister indiscriminately begins casting demons out of a person. And while this may provide some measure of relief, it does not solve the root issue.

This can be likened to a person that has severe Degenerative arthritis in their hip. They experience chronic and severe pain on a daily basis. They walk with a limp and are unable to function in life in a normal manner due to their disability. Rather than having a total hip replacement surgery where the deteriorated bone and cartilage is removed and replaced, they may opt for a cortisone injection. While this may alleviate the pain on temporary basis, it is not removing the causative issue.

For comprehensive deliverance, the demons must be cast out and the strongman, or the ruling principality that heads these demons, must be bound – First! There is a biblical order in which this must be done. When it is not followed, we find that people experience complete deliverance because the demons were bound, but the strongman is allowed to stay.

Bind the Strongman First

Jesus said bind the strongman first.

*No man can enter into a strong man's house, and spoil his goods, except he will **first** bind the strong man; and then he will spoil his house. – Mark 3:27 (KJV)*

Jesus gave us very important keys regarding deliverance ministry; Jesus said ......

1. *"No man can enter into a strongman's house"*
2. *"You can't spoil the Strongman's goods, ... <u>unless you first bind him."</u>*

- **Enter** – *eiserchomai*; to take possession of the thoughts that come into the mind.

- **Strongman** – *ischyros;* strong either in body or in mind. The strongman is the ruling and controlling demonic principality over a network of demons."

- **Strongman's House** – *oikia;* an inhabited edifice, a dwelling, the inmates of a house, the family, property, wealth and goods. "The strong-man's house is the Soul (mind, will & emotions) of the person that is bound (i.e. host)"

- **Spoil** – *diarpazō;* to seize or plunder his goods. "To occupy a territory or take back property."

- **Goods** – *skeuos*; equipment, armament of vessels, shield. "The strongman's goods represent the demons that surround and protect the ruling principality.

- **First** – *prōton;* firstly (in time, place, order, or importance).

- **Bind** - *deō*; to stop, forbid, prohibit and prevent.

Why are we told to bind him? Why not cast him out?

Rules of Engagement

As in any military campaign, one of the first rules of engagement is to immobilize and take out the enemy's communication network. Destroying communication systems like Telephone lines, Internet fiber optics and transport systems are especially important. While this is a natural example, it applies in similar fashion in the spiritual arena.

As previously discussed, many people are severely bound because they believe the lies of the enemy. This is termed the 'stronghold.' Over time, lesser demons will scout

out the stronghold to determine if it's fortified enough to support the strongman. If it is, lesser demons of select characteristics will begin to torment the host. The reason for this is that these demons need to attack the persons will. The most effective method of doing this is through a strategic campaign of consistent mental and emotional attacks that have the host normalize their unstable behavior. As the dysfunction is normalize, the person's "will' is pacified to where the impending strongman will go undetected.

When the host has been bound for many years, and has normalized their dysfunction, they have come into agreement with the demonic bondage, and the strongman is permitted to enter deep into the soul.

Therefore, the reason we must bind the strongman first, is to stop the ruling principality from orchestrating its demonic network and stop all communication to its demonic henchmen.

Truth will always agitate the strongman and cause him to re-position his demons to protect his house. For example, a strongman of Rejection, when exposed to the truth may manifest 'retaliation' or 'withdrawal.'

If we focus solely on casting out that which the Strongman manifested (revealed) without FIRST binding the Strongman, his ability to maintain his operation within the Stronghold never ceases and the deception continues. At best, the deliverance candidate may experience minor or temporary relief, but not lasting freedom. It's critical that the Strongman is neutralized so that further expansion does not occur within the stronghold developed in ones mind.

When the Kingdom of God is preached it will "bind" the Kingdom of Darkness from having control over one's mind and liberate the captives.

However, the "binding" of the controlling strongman is only temporary. It simply enables the deliverance minister to begin to breakdown and remove the protective shield of the lesser demons. At this point in the deliverance process, the strong man may not be ejected, but he is prohibited from disseminating further directives to his demonic forces.

In Mark 3:27, Jesus is basically saying, don't let the strongman have the ability to communicate to his demonic network. You must first bind him." When you bind someone, you limit his influence or his threat. That's what binding will do - it will stop the strongman from influencing your life.

Identifying the Strongman

To identify who the strongman is, requires spiritual discernment and cutting edge training. Spiritual discernment always comes before training. Deliverance training and education is very important to have but must be viewed as a supplement to the gift of spiritual discernment.

.... to another discerning of spirits I Corinthians 12:10

However, there are some key indicators that will assist the deliverance minister to properly identifying the strongman.

For example if a person suffers from sickness, disease, an ailment, disability, chronic pain or some terminal illness, then the strongman called the "Spirit of Infirmity" should be bound.

Another example would be if a person suffers from anxiety, phobias, compulsive behavior patterns, ADHD, OCD, PTSD, insomnia or scary nightmares, then the strongman called the "Spirit of Fear" should be bound.

Names of Strongman

Lying Spirit	Jeremiah 23: 14 - *"They commit adultery and walk in the spirit of lies"*
Spirit of Divination	Acts 16:16 – *"as we went to prayer, a certain damsel possessed with a spirit of divination met us,"*
Spirit of Jealousy	Number 5:14 – *"or if the spirit of jealousy comes upon him"*
Perverse Spirit	Matthew 15:19 – *"Out of the mind come evil thoughts, murder, adultery, sexual sins, stealing, lying, and speaking evil of others."*
Spirit of Haughtiness	Proverbs 16:18 – *"Pride goeth before destruction, and an haughty spirit before a fall"*
Spirit of Whoredoms	Hosea 5:4 – *"for the spirit of whoredoms is in the midst of them,"*
Spirit of Infirmity	Luke 13:11 – *"there was a woman which had a spirit of infirmity eighteen years"*
Deaf & Dumb Spirit	Mark 9:25 – *"Thou dumb and deaf spirit, I charge thee, come out of him"*
Spirit of Anti-Christ	I John 4:3 – *"And every spirit that confesseth not that Jesus Christ is come in the flesh is not of God: and this is that spirit of antichrist"*
Spirit of Error	I John 4:6 – *"Hereby know we the spirit of truth, and the spirit of error"*
Spirit of Bondage	Romans 8:15 – *"For ye have not received the spirit of bondage"*
Spirit of Fear	II Timothy 1:7 – *"For God hath not given us the spirit of fear;"*

Familiar Spirit	Leviticus 19:31 - *"Give no regard to mediums and familiar spirits; do not seek after them, to be defiled by them"*
Spirit of Heaviness	Isaiah 61:3 - *The garment of praise for the spirit of heaviness;*
Seducing Spirit	I Timothy 4:1 – *"Now the Spirit speaketh expressly, that in the latter times some shall depart from the faith, giving heed to seducing spirits"*
Spirit of Death	Hebrews 2:14 – *"that through death he might destroy him that had the power of death, that is, the devil"*

Dismantling the Network

Once you stop the strongman from communicating to his network of demons, begin to call out demonic characteristics tied to that strongman grouping. This will start the process of dismantling the strongman's network.

For example, if the strongman classified as the "Spirit of Error" is bound, one should immediately begin to rout out evil spirits of; religion, tradition, legalism, hypocrisy, deception, racism, prejudice, hatred, murdering spirits, denominationalism, self-righteous spirits etc.

This will have a devastating effect on the strongman as the light of God begins to manifest in the life of the host. The more demons that can be eradicated from the host, the greater the torment. This is referred to as "dividing up the goods" or "spoiling the goods."

When the strong man, fully armed, [from his courtyard] guards his own dwelling, his belongings are undisturbed [his property is at peace and is secure]. But when one stronger than he attacks him and conquers him, he robs him of his whole armor on which he had relied and divides up and distributes all his goods as plunder – Luke 11:21-22 Amplified Version

Remember, the Strongman relies on his goods to protect him. The goods (demons) shield, cover-up and enable the strongman to remain in the dark.

As demons are cast out they become tormented. The same holds true for the strongman. Once evicted from "his house," he is sent to a place of dryness. When the Strongman leaves, he is tormented, but the host has peace.

When He had come to the other side, to the country of the Gergesenes, there met Him two demon-possessed men, coming out of the tombs, exceedingly fierce, so that no one could pass that way. And suddenly they cried out, saying, "What have we to do with You, Jesus, You Son of God? Have You come here to torment us before the time?" – Matthew 8:28-10

Post-Deliverance

Once you have been set free it is critical to maintain your deliverance. The demonic spirits and strongman will make every attempt to come back to their "home".

"When an impure spirit comes out of a person, it goes through arid places seeking rest and does not find it. Then it says, 'I will return to the house I left.' When it arrives, it finds the house unoccupied, swept clean and put in order. Then it goes and takes with it seven other spirits more wicked than itself, and they go in and live there. And the final condition of that person is worse than the first. That is how it will be with this wicked generation." - Matthew 12:43-45.

The key to real freedom and overcoming the strongman is to displace the enemy and establish the presence of God. One of the greatest ways we can plunder the strongman's house and overcome the enemy's power is by understanding our true authority in Christ and how to resist the devil by submitting to God's promises.

Deliverance is a continuous process in the life of every born again believer.

Deliverance is the children's bread and should be consumed daily.

Once demons and the strongman are cast out, it is vitally important for the host to begin to renew their Mind.

And do not be conformed to this world, but be transformed by the renewing of your mind, that you may prove what is that good and acceptable and perfect will of God. – Romans 12:2

God's Word is deliverance. Meditating on the Word of God and seeing yourself as a new creation will uproot all strongholds in the mind, will and emotions.

He sent His word and healed them, And delivered them from their destructions. – Psalms 107:20

It is the word of God that cleanses the Body and Soul from sickness, diseases and demonic hindrances. It is essential to maintain your deliverance by eating the bread of deliverance.

When one gets delivered from demonic spirits, there is a responsibility on the person's part to cast down imagination and take their thought life captive. This will remove any pre-existing strongholds in the Soul.

Matt 12:43-45 gives us a clear understanding about when an unclean spirit is cast out and returns to the house (stronghold), and it is found clean, swept, and empty.

"When an unclean spirit goes out of a man, he goes through dry places, seeking rest, and finds none. Then he says, 'I will return to my house from which I came.' And when he comes, he finds it empty, swept, and put in order. Then he goes and takes with him seven other spirits more wicked than himself, and they enter and dwell there; and the last state of that man is worse than the first. So shall it also be with this wicked generation." – Matthew 12:43-45

The term "clean, swept and empty" is a clear indication that the host has not changed their thought patterns or renewed their mind.

It's an unfortunate reality that many believers have demons cast out of them, only to have them return in greater force. The primary reason for this is because they're not disciples of the Lord. They may be believers, but they are not disciples.

Disciples are committed to obeying that which the Lord commanded.

A believer may be an uncommitted soul simply looking for a way out of hell, yet is unwilling to be held accountable to the renewing of their mind through the word of God. This is why many, after going through deliverance they return to their past mess, issues and dysfunction.

Believers must read the Word of God and fill their house (mind, will and emotions) with it. You can't get delivered, then continue to attend a fellowship where you're just preached at and think that's all that's needed to stay free. You must fill your temple daily with God's Word, be obedient and submit your will to The King and His Kingdom.

Derek Prince in his book entitled "They Shall Expel Demons," lists the following principles to be followed after deliverance.

- Live by God's Word.
- Put on the garment of praise.
- Come under discipline.
- Cultivate right fellowship.
- Be filled with the Holy Spirit.
- Make sure you have passed through the water of baptism.
- Put on the whole armour of God.

To put on the whole armour of God, is to put on Gods word. This is not speaking of putting it on your spirit man, but rather to arm your Soul (mind, will and emotions) with it. Consider, your newly created spirit was born from the Word of God. Peter 1:23 says.....

"having been born again, not of corruptible seed but incorruptible, through the word of God which lives and abides forever."

Therefore your spirit man and the Word are one. It's your mind that must be renewed to enjoy lasting deliverance and healing.

Remember .... "as a man thinks, so is he"

Conclusion

The Strongman is the ruling principality, the leader of the demonic pack. His desire is to remain hidden as he coordinates a deep level of bondage in a person's life, rendering them in a state hopelessness, despair and dysfunction. Believers must FIRST bind the strongman and cast out demons, ultimately driving out the strongman. Renewing the mind is the critical component for tearing down all remaining strongholds in the mind. This will lead to a victorious life.

Section Notes:

_____

_____

_____

_____

_____

_____

_____

Section Four
How to Deal with the Mind

Dealing with the Mind

Since you have been told that demons do exist and that they would like to take up residence in your soul. You must know what you are required by the Father to do about your mind. Man's Soul consists of the Mind, Will and Emotions (senses).

The mind is the organ of thought. The mind is the part of the soul that thinks.

In my book, The Freedom Series - Deliverance for the Mind©, I talk about the fact that if we were told how to think we would have no problem with Satan or demons. In fact, we are told in God's word how to think. God has given the citizens of the Kingdom the keys on how and what to think. Consider just a few verses that speak to this.

Finally, brethren, whatever things are true, whatever things are noble, whatever things are just, whatever things are pure, whatever things are lovely, whatever things are of good report, if there is any virtue and if there is anything praiseworthy— meditate on these things – Philippians 4:8

Set your mind on things above, not on things on the earth. – Colossians 3:2

Do not curse the king, even in your thought; - Ecclesiastes10:20

Let this mind be in you which was also in Christ Jesus ... - Philippians 2:5

The demonic cannot stay in the light. They love darkness because their deeds are ungodly. Their intentions are to stop you from operating in whom God has made you. You will become what you think. You can never go where you do not first see yourself going.

Proverbs 23:7 tells us, *"For as he thinketh in his heart, so is he."* A man's life is a result of his thinking.

Your imagination is your spiritual womb. It is the place of conception for your life's journey. This is the place where words or imaginations are conceived and subsequently grow.

In like fashion, consider the female's womb being the place where the baby grows. It is within the womb that the baby is formed into what it is going to be. At the appointed time, the baby is born. It is within the womb that you became the physical person. In the womb, you received your physical distinctions.

Now let's compare this with the mind. The mind is the womb of your destiny. If you can understand that the physical womb is the place we are formed, then you can understand that the mind is also the place where we are formed. The mind is where we will excel or fail in getting to our destiny. It is in the mind where you become that person you think you are. It is in your mind that what is spoken and conceived that you become. This is why the scripture instructs us to teach our children the word, and speak it over them at all times. Hearing and seeing the word of God will transform you into the image the Heavenly Father who created you.

What you put off or out of your mind, such as the works of darkness, will leave you. Only when you put off the darkness, can you then put on your mind the Armour of light, which is God's word. Once this is accomplished you will become who you are meant to be according to the Word of God.

The night is far spent, the day is at hand: let us therefore cast off the works of darkness, and let us put on the armour of light - Romans 13:12 (KJV)

Lie not one to another, seeing that ye have put off the old man with his deeds; - Colossians 3:9 (KJV)

That is why we have been told in the word of God to start depositing the word in our children when they are young. They will not let it go when they are old. It is meant to shape their life and develop them into the dynamic individuals they're created to be. The Word of God is to lead them as they yield to it. The word will guide them to righteous living and peace with God.

Train up a child in the way he should go; even when he is old he will not depart from it. –Proverbs 22:6 (ESV)

You shall teach them to your children, talking of them when you are sitting in your house and when you are walking by the way, and when you lie down and when you rise. -Deuteronomy 11:19 (ESV)

He established a testimony in Jacob and appointed a law in Israel, which he commanded our fathers to teach to their children, that the next generation might know them, the children yet unborn, and arise and tell them to their children, so that they should set their hope in God and not forget the works of God but keep his commandments. - Psalms 78:5-7 (ESV)

Discipline your son, and he will give you rest; he will give delight to your heart. - Proverbs 29:17

Fathers, do not provoke your children to anger, but bring them up in the discipline and instruction of the Lord. - Ephesians 6:4

Behold, children are a heritage from the Lord, The fruit of the womb is a reward. Like arrows in the hand of a warrior, So are the children of one's youth. Happy is the man who has his quiver full of them; They shall not be ashamed, But shall speak with their enemies in the gate. – Psalms 127:3-5

Hearing God voice vs. other voices

You can expect to hear many voices that seek to lead you astray from the sound doctrine and teaching of the Bible. We are surrounded with many voices; the voice that we obey can determine our eternal destiny.

- Judas heard Satan's voice and betrayed Jesus. He ultimately perished and committed suicide.

- Peter heard Satan's voice and did not believe the voice of Jesus. - Peter got rebuked and soon afterward denied the Lord Jesus.

- The high priest heard Satan's voice and believed Jesus was speaking blasphemy, when Jesus said He was the Son of the Moist high. It may have cost him his eternal destiny.

- Jesus healed the leper and told him to say nothing to any man. However, the leper heard Satan's voice and disobeyed the voice of the one that healed him. As a result, the bible tells us that Jesus could do no more enter into the city.

- Pontius Pilate was determined to let Jesus go; however the wild voices of the angry mob influenced him to do otherwise.

Satan's voice will put lying thoughts in your mind, which goes against God's Word. The lies of the enemy will tell you that you are not loved, worthy or worse yet, that you don't need God.

Which voice do you hear?

We were created to yield and be guided by the voice of God. In the Garden of Eden, Eve was introduced to another voice. When she began to listen to another voice it challenged the voice of God. It tempted her to reason why God said what he said. This enticement was not the voice of God. This voice was the voice of the enemy. God came to speak to Adam and Eve everyday in the evening. If there was a question or concern about God's directives why not ask Him. Eve's deception was to reason instead of asking the Father.

But I fear, lest somehow, as the serpent deceived Eve by his craftiness, so your minds may be corrupted from the simplicity that is in Christ. – 2 Corinthians 11:3

The voice of the serpent had several intentions:

1. To get the Man of God to look in himself for the answers and the solutions for what comes his way.

2. To get the Man of God to desire or lust for what he thought he should have.

3. To sever communication with the Father by tempting you to get directions from someone else, whether it is one's reasoning or demonic intervention.

In either case, you are not yielding your life to the Father to guide you in what is best for you. The sole purpose of the enemy's voice was to get him to desire something that the Creator did not intend for him. Satan's plan is to get us to mind or be concerned about the things of man therefore giving him an entrance in our lives.

In Mark Chapter 8, we see an example of this. Peter began to rebuke Jesus when he began to teach them about his sufferings, how he would be rejected of the elders, and of the chief priests, and scribes, and be killed, and after three days rise again. We see what Jesus thought of Peter when he rebuked Satan.

But when he had turned about and looked on his disciples, he rebuked Peter, saying, Get thee behind me Satan: for thou savourest not the things that be of God, but the things that be of men. And when he had called the people unto him with his disciples also, he said unto them, Whosoever will come after me, let him deny himself, and take up his cross, and follow me. For whosoever will save his life shall lose it; but whosoever shall lose his life for my sake and the gospel's, the same shall save it. For what shall it profit a man, if he shall gain the whole world, and lose his own soul?
Mark 8:33-36

Satan is analogous to the darkness. The darkness in our minds is the deception and ignorance of who we are in Christ- our True Identity. The only way to destroy the darkness in our mind is by Light. God's word is the light and it is truth. God and the Devil are diametrically opposed. Like light and darkness, they are enemies.

In Acts 26 God told Paul, *"I will rescue you from your own people and from the Gentiles. I am sending you to them to open their eyes and turn them from darkness to light, and from the power of Satan to God."*

Paul's ministry was, "To open their (our) eyes, and to turn them from darkness to light, and from the power of Satan unto God."

Satan gets the advantage when we allow him to cast his fiery darts of deception into our minds.

Renewing your mind to this New Life

Our Father knows that becoming as little children has its purpose in fulfilling what he has for us and that is Kingdom living.

The Amplified version of the Bible in Matthew 18:3-6 says:

"I assure you and most solemnly say to you, unless you repent [that is, change your inner self—your old way of thinking, live changed lives] and become like children [trusting, humble, and forgiving], you will never enter the kingdom of heaven. Therefore, whoever humbles himself like this child is greatest in the kingdom of heaven. Whoever receives and welcomes one child like this in My name receives Me; but whoever causes one of these little ones who believe in Me to stumble and sin [by leading him away from My teaching], it would be better for him to have a heavy millstone [as large as one turned by a donkey] hung around his neck and to be drowned in the depth of the sea."

Here's what you must understand. If you were not taught the word of God as a child, you must go back and become like a child. It's not that you need to be a child, but rather take on the like-kind attributes of a child to humble yourself, be teachable and receive God's word and apply it without question.

Satan wants to distract many from their destiny and purpose, and from the Fathers will for us.

Satan knows that the most vulnerable time is when we are young. He knows that if he can stop us when we are children, we will not be able to carry out our purpose. We must teach our children how to deal with Satan and his deceptive lies.

To distort or destroy a child's value, Satan attacks in 4 specific areas.

Here are 4 darts that can stunt or ruin a child's Godly value:

- Rejection
- Abandonment
- Molestation
- Abuse

The purpose of these darts is so that the enemy with his world system can divert and hinder the plan of God for our lives. He tries do destroy us when we are young. It is so important that we are protected with God's word while we are young. Remember the scripture has told us that when we are taught the word we will not depart from it when we are old. We are to be shielded by the Word of God given to us by parents or guardians. If we're not then we will grow up, thinking like the enemy. We will be lured to the world and it systems to find the answers. The world will tell you that it is the good life. But all its skills can only offer death, lack, fear and destruction.

This I say, therefore, and testify in the Lord, that you should no longer walk as the rest of the Gentiles walk, in the futility of their mind, having their understanding darkened, being alienated from the life of God, because of the ignorance that is in

*them, because of the blindness of their heart; who, being past feeling, have given themselves over to lewdness, to work all uncleanness with greediness.
But you have not so learned Christ, if indeed you have heard Him and have been taught by Him, as the truth is in Jesus: that you <u>put off</u>, concerning your former conduct, the old man which grows corrupt according to the deceitful lusts, and be renewed in the spirit of your mind, and that you <u>put on</u> the new man which was created according to God, in true righteousness and holiness. – Ephesians 4:17-24*

There are decisions that we must make as born again Kingdom citizens. The decision of putting off the former conversation or lifestyle, and putting on the new man or new life will transform you.

Wherefore seeing we also are compassed about with so great a cloud of witnesses, let us lay aside every weight, and the sin which doth so easily beset us, and let us run with patience the race that is set before us – Heb. 12:1

Therefore I exhort you, brothers and sisters, by the mercies of God, to present your bodies as a sacrifice – alive, holy, and pleasing to God-which is your reasonable service. Do not conformed to this present world, but be transformed by the renewing of your mind, so that you may test and approve what is the will of God- what is good and well-pleasing and perfect. Romans 12:1-2

What to "Put-on / Put-off"

Christians often fail to change because they attempt to change solely by breaking bad habits. However, change that lasts will not take place until one replaces the bad habit with a godly habit. Ephesians 4:22-24 explains this as the "Principle of Replacement." This process of change is described in the Bible by the terms "Put-Off, Renew, and Put-On."

Strong's Greek Concordance word and definition

Put Off (Greek) *Apotithemi* - to lay aside, take off, to strip off from oneself denoting separation from what is put off, renounce, stow away.

Put on (Greek) *endyō* - to endue, array, clothe with,

From *en* and *duno* (in the sense of sinking into a garment); to invest with clothing
en (a preposition) – properly, in (inside, within); (figuratively) "in the realm (sphere) of," as in the condition (state) in which something operates from the inside (within).

Christians are to Put Off the old sinful way of life; renew their mind with Biblical truth, and Put On the new godly way of life.

It has been found that you cannot break a habit. You must replace it with something else. Consequently the habit will die due to lack of attention, life or strength.

The bible tells us in Romans 12:2 to Renew our mind. To do so, one must be deliberate and exercise control over what is put into it.

Additionally, all toxic thoughts and imaginations need to be removed or "Put-Off." This is a tool for you to use so that you make decisions that are life and not death. When you choose the word you choose life and when you walk after things of the flesh and the world system you choose death. It is important that you understand that every decision has a consequence. When we are obeying the Lord by choosing His word, we enable the blessings of God to come because we call them to us by our choice to go with God.

Study these scriptures and make a definite decision to apply them to your life daily. They will transform you. You will find that the more you choose life the easier it will be to live by them. Do not be concerned as to how the change will occur, just put off what the word tells you to and then put on the Word of God. This is how we overcome the world.

Here is a list of things we should Put off and Put on:

Put-on / Put-off - Listing

"Put Off"	Scriptural Insight	"Put On"	Scriptural Insight
Lack of Love	1 John 4:7,8,20	Love	John 15:12
Judging	Matt 7:1-2	Let God search my Heart	John 8:9 John 15:22
Bitterness	Heb. 12:15	Tenderhearted and Forgiving	Eph. 4:32
Unforgiving Spirit	Mark 11:26	Forgiving spirit	Col. 3:13
Selfishness	Phil. 2:21	John 12:24	Self Denial
Pride	Prov. 16:5	James 4:6	Humility
Boasting (Conceit)	1 Cor. 4;7	Phil. 2:3	Esteeming Others
Stubbornness	1 Samuel 15:23	Brokenness	Romans 6:13
Disrespect for Authority	Acts 23:5	Honor Authority	Heb. 13:17
Rebellion	1 Samuel 15:23	Submission	Heb. 13:17
Disobedience	1 Samuel 12:15	Obedience	Deut. 11:27
Impatience	James 1:2-4	Patience	Heb. 10:36
Ungratefulness	Romans 1:21	Gratefulness	Eph. 5:20
Murmuring/ Complaining	Phil. 2:14	Praise	Heb. 13:15
Covetousness	Luke 12:15	Contentment	Heb. 13:5

Discontent	Heb. 13:5	Contentment	1 Tim. 6:8
Irritation of others	Gal. 5:26	Preferring in love	Phil.2:3-4
Jealousy	Gal. 5:26	Trust	1 Cor. 13:4
Strife/Contention	Prov. 13:10	Peace	James 3:17
Retaliation	Prov. 24;29	Return good for evil	Rom. 12:19-20
Losing temper	Prov. 25:28	Self-control	Prov. 16:32
Anger	Prov. 29:22	Self-control	Gal. 5:22-23
Wrath	James 1:19-20	Soft Answer	Prov. 15:1
Easily irritated	1 Cor. 13:5	Not easily provoked	Prov. 19:11
Hatred	Matt. 5:21-22	Love	1 Cor. 13:3
Murder	Exodus 20:13	Love	Romans 13:10
Gossip	1 Tim.5:13	Edifying speech	Eph. 4:29
Evil speaking	James 4:11	Good Report	Prov. 15:20
Critical spirit	Gal. 5:15	Kindness	Col. 3:12
Lying	Eph. 4:25	Speak Truth	Zec. 8;16
Profanity	Prov. 4:24	Pure Speech	Prov. 15:4
Idle Words	Matt. 12:36	Bridle tongue	Prov. 21:23
Wrong motives	1 Sam. 16:7	Spiritual Motives	1 Cor. 10:31
Evil Thoughts	Matt. 5:19-20	Pure Thoughts	Phil4:8
Complacency	Rev. 3:15	Zeal	Rev. 3:19
Laziness	Prov. 20:4	Diligence	Prov. 6:6-11
Slothfulness	Prov. 18:9	Wholeheartedness	Col. 3:23
Hypocrisy	Job 8:13	Sincerity	1 Thess. 2:3
Idolatry	Deut. 11:16	Worship only God	Col. 1:18
Left first Love	Rev. 2:4	Fervent Devotion	Rev. 2:5
Lack in rejoicing	Phil. 4:4	Rejoicing always	1 Thess. 5:18
Worry/fear	Matt. 6:25-32	Trust	1 Peter 5:7
Unbelief	Heb. 3:12	Faith	Heb. 11:1,6
Unfaithfulness	Prov. 25:19	Faithfulness	Luke 16:10-12
Neglect study of the Bible	2 Tim. 3:14-17	Study of the Bible/Meditation	Psa. 1:2
Prayerlessness	Luke 18:1	Praying	Matt. 26:41
No burden for the lost	Matt. 9:36-38	Witnessing/compassion	Acts 1:8
Burying Talents	Luke 12:48	Developing abilities	1 Cor. 4:2
Irresponsibility for Family / Work	Luke 16:12	Responsibility	Luke 16:10
Procrastination	Prov. 10:5	Diligence	Prov. 27:1
Irreverence in Church	Eccl. 5:1	Reverence	Psa. 89:7
Inhospitable	1 Peter 4:9	Hospitable	Rom. 12:13
Cheating	2 Cor. 4:2	Honesty	2 Cor. 8:21
Stealing	Prov. 29:24	Working/Giving	Eph. 4:28
Lack of Moderation	Prov. 11:1	Temperance	I Cor. 9:25
Gluttony	Prov. 23:21	Discipline	1 Cor. 9:27

Wrong Friends	Psa. 1:1	Godly Friends	Prov. 13:20
Temporal Values	Matt. 6:19-21	Eternal Value	2 Cor. 4:18
Love of Money/Greed	1 Tim. 6:9-10	Love God	Matt. 6:33
Stinginess	1 John 3:17	Generosity	Prov. 11:24-25
Moral Impurity	1 Thess. 4:7	Moral purity	1 Thess. 4:4
Fornication	1 Cor. 6:18	Abstinence	1 Thess. 4:3
Lust	1 Peter 2:11	Pure Desires	Titus 2:12
Adultery	Matt. 5:27	Marital Fidelity	Prov. 5:14-19
Homosexuality	Lev. 18:22	Moral Purity	1 Thess. 4:-5
Incest	Lev. 18:6	Moral Purity	1 Cor. 7:2, 5
Pornography	Psa. 101:3	Pure Thoughts	Phil. 4:8
Immodest Dress	Prov. 7:10	Modesty	1 Tim. 2:9
Flirtation	Prov. 7:21	Gentle, quiet spirit	1 Peter 3:4
Worldly entertainment	Prov. 21:17	Spiritual Pursuits	Gal. 5:16
Fleshy music	Eph. 4:29-30	Edifying Music	Eph. 5:19
Bodily harm	1 Cor. 3:16-17	Glorify God in body	1 Cor. 6:19-20
Alcoholism	Prov. 20:1	Abstinence	Prov. 23:30

Conclusion

The Warfare against the Kingdom of Darkness, Satan, his fallen angels and demons, begins and ends in our mind. The key to winning the battle is through obedience to God's Word and doing the work. That work, is Putting off the old ways of thinking, and Putting on the New Man.

Section Notes:

Section Five
Common Misconceptions of Deliverance Ministry

Common Misconceptions

Deliverance was a core ministry of the Lord Jesus Christ. Whether the oppressed person was a mute boy who suffered from seizures [Mark 9:14-25] or a demoniac man who had been driven from his community [Luke 8:29], Jesus was sent to liberate those who were oppressed [Luke 4:18]. This is the heart of deliverance ministry. After his ascension, this vital ministry was passed on to the apostles and his disciples. Like those early believers, we are instructed in scripture to cast out demons.

Today, we find a mixed mindset when it comes to the topic of deliverance. Even among church leaders this fundamental ministry is often viewed as either obsolete or as having been replaced by the more common "counseling sessions." Clearly, not everyone embraces deliverance ministry, specifically the casting out of demons.

Having been engaged in deliverance ministry for several years, we can testify of the tremendous need for this ministry to be active in the lives of all believers. Many people are coming out of the occult, witchcraft, spiritualism, and the New Age movement and into our churches. Others come in seeking help with emotional issues and wounds that have built up over decades.

The church and specifically its leaders must be properly trained in the area of deliverance to provide solutions to these problems. Deliverance ministry is a ministry of compassion that places the finger of God on a person's life and emancipates them from the pain of their past, and delivers them into the reality of who they are in Christ. There simply is no greater joy that comes to our heart than to see a person who has been emotionally wounded or mentally bound, become liberated from torment, agony and pain.

Before we can see this ministry excel within the Body of Christ, we need to eliminate some of the misconceptions that exist.

Misconception – "Deliverance Ministry is only for Leaders"

Casting out demons (or deliverance ministry) is not an exclusive ministry that only a few have. While it is true that we all operate in varying degrees of anointing and gifting, every believer needs to be equipped to perform basic deliverance.

In Mark 16 Jesus appeared to His apostles and said *"And these signs shall follow them that believe; In my name shall they cast out devils; they shall speak with new tongues; They shall take up serpents; and if they drink any deadly thing, it shall not hurt them; they shall lay hands on the sick, and they shall recover."*

From the above scripture it is evident that a "believer", not necessarily a leader, is to cast out devils. If that was not the case then one could make the argument that only leaders should speak in new tongues or lay hands on the sick.

In surveying the landscape of the church, however, it is not difficult to see that many believers today cannot recognize the presence of demons or strongholds in their life or the lives of others. If they can, they typically lack the training necessary to get the people that are in bondage free from the enemy's tactics. They usually become frustrated and ultimately bring the one in bondage to leadership for a solution.

Misconception – "Leaders do not need to be equipped in Deliverance"

Unfortunately the lack of equipping in the area of deliverance ministry is not unique to the sheep but is prevalent among the shepherds as well. We can attest to this by the sheer volume of people that seek out our ministry for deliverance. The most common answer we get when we ask them "why they came to us," is that their Pastor or church does not have a deliverance ministry and/or does not believe in casting out demons.

In Ephesians chapter 4, we see that the Lord gave 5 gifts to the Body of Christ for the purpose of *"equipping of the saints for the work of ministry."* Since every believer has been commanded to cast out demons, it is only reasonable to ascertain that the ones doing the equipping need to be skilled in the area themselves. Leaders have a responsibility to get the believer equipped whether by their ministry or by reaching out to other leaders who have the revelation and expertise in this specific area. As leaders we must provide a "well-balanced" diet of Kingdom truth and applications. Deliverance ministry is no exception. Leaders must remain teachable and receive quality training also.

Without proper deliverance training we run the risk of opening the door to spiritual warfare tactics that are esoteric, bizarre, and flaky. There is probably no other area of ministry that has been more sensationalized than deliverance and spiritual warfare.

A quality deliverance minister is one that is well trained and understands his or her vocation. They understand the complexities of the deliverance process and can assess emotional issues and wounds that have built up over decades.

Engaging in deliverance ministry without proper training can bring more harm than good.

As minister's who focus on deliverance, we've often encountered individuals who desperately wanted and believed that they could be delivered from bondage, but they had been disappointed in the past by ministers who had not been properly trained. Poorly trained leaders attempt to provide deliverance by throwing anointing oil or some other fleshly tactic instead of engaging in genuine deliverance ministry.

Misconception –"Deliverance will frighten people and they will leave the Church"

In actuality we have found just the opposite to be true. People need and want deliverance. Once the word gets out that there is a place for people to truly receive their deliverance, your ministry will grow – exponentially.

Today, many leaders talk of diminishing attendance and a lack of true power in their services. To compensate for this, many have focused on creating programs or an environment that is "seeker-friendly" or "culturally relevant." The *dynamis* - that miraculous power for which we so passionately pray - is replaced by energetic bands, digitalized lighting systems, and fog machines. Certainly there is nothing wrong with state of the art technology, but it is a fraudulent substitute for the miraculous power of God.

In the 1st century people clustered to Jesus because He was a problem solver. He eliminated an issue that a woman had for 18 years. He solved the problem of a frustrated father whose son was stricken with seizures and convulsions. Jesus brought the miracle-working power of God into people's lives, and once word travelled that they could get free from years of agony, His meetings got so big that His family couldn't get in the service. In one meeting the roof had to be torn apart just to get in. When is the last time that happened at your service?

> Now John answered Him, saying, "Teacher, we saw someone who does not follow us casting out demons in Your name, and we forbade him because he does not follow us." But Jesus said, "Do not forbid him, for no one who works a miracle in My name can soon afterward speak evil of Me." - Mark 9:38-39

Casting out demons is supernatural and the manifestation of a miracle. Miracles solve problems and we need leaders that can solve problems using Kingdom tactics. Jesus demonstrated the kingdom of God by driving demons out of people's lives.

People spend billions of dollars trying to get free from sickness, disease, addictions, and emotional issues. Deliverance ministry solves the problems of mankind. The church needs to be the spiritual hospital, urgent care, emergency room, surgical center, and recovery room for the oppressed.

Because deliverance is a hands-on ministry, it is a practical way to shift people from sitting lethargically in pews to actively participating in spiritual warfare. Being involved in deliverance ministry will grow your church because people want solutions to their problems.

Misconception – "Demons can jump on you"

The short answer is no. There's nowhere in Scripture where we see demons jumping from one person to another. Again, while this belief may have people gravitating to another esoteric teaching, there's simply just no scriptural support for this concept. We do see in the word of God however that Jesus did permit demons to come out of a man and go into the swine. But once again, demons do not have the authority to do whatever they want. There needs to be an open door or access point for them to enter in.

Misconception – "Demons are in Objects"

There are many people and certainly much teaching around this statement, however, once again, there is no support within the word of God, specifically in the New Testament, that gives verification to this manifestation. That's not to say that evil spirits do not gravitate around objects, artifacts, Jewelry, statues or other paraphernalia that has been used as a tool of idolatry or pagan worship.

There is no biblical support to the idea that demons can attach themselves to physical objects. This belief is actually part of superstitious practices and occult beliefs found among those who practice the occult. Although, many eastern religions and the occult use artifacts in their method of worship, for example Buddha or the Greek goddess Diana, the objects in and of themselves have no demonic spirit in them.

Demons are spirits and a spirit does not inhabit animate objects. This belief is what's called animism. Animism is the belief that everything has a soul or spirit, an *anima* in Latin, including animals, plants, rocks, mountains, rivers, and stars.

We do believe that an object can be considered an unclean thing, however this speaks more about the person that has the object rather than the object itself. If a person is demonically bound and has a stronghold in the mind, they are the one that has the evil spirit in them in the object is simply nothing more than a point of contact for them. This also addresses is another common misconception that "Demon's can be transferred by touching something evil." It simply not true. If that were the case, then when Jesus permitted the woman that was the prostitute to touch him, then why do we not see demons transferring to Jesus? Wasn't that woman evil?

Misconception - "Demons operate in people illegally"

Perhaps you've heard it said before – "devil your operating in that person illegally."

Actually, that's not true. Satan or his demons do not have the power to override a person's will. For a demon to enter into a person there must be an open access point. Demons cannot bully their way into a person.

God has given each one of us a free will and He will never violate that free will. When we desire Jesus to come into our lives, we have to be willing to give Him our direct permission to be able to do so. God will never force Himself on anyone.

In like manner, demons cannot enter a person unless they willingly do or think something evil. That opens up the door for demons to come in and demonize a person.

Your will gives demon their legal right to bind you.

A legal right is something that can give demons an opportunity to enter or harass us, or gives them the right to remain in us even when we try to cast them out.

Demons are at work in the sons of disobedience (*Eph 2:2*). Those who disobey God are giving demons a right to operate in them. This applies also to Christians and unbelievers. In the book of Acts, Peter stated that Satan had filled the heart of Ananias. Ananias lied and said that he was giving to God more than he really was. Therefore, anyone who is lying could have his or her heart filled by Satan.
Paul told the believers in Ephesus: *"Neither give place to the devil"* (Eph 4:27). This implies that it is possible for a born-again, spirit filled believer to give place to the devil.

Giving place to the devil is giving him legal rights.

Misconception – "Demons attack your Money"

Here's another false misconception and certainly one that many people subscribe to when they are going through financial hardships. No, it is not true. Demons do not attack your money, your wallet or your checkbook. People have problems financially because they are not good stewards of the money God has blessed them with. Consider that the average person does not have a working budget. Most people don't even have financial goals. Others spend frivolously and accumulate enormous amounts of Debt. They have no accountability and accept no responsibility for their financial situation; rather they indiscriminately blame their financial woes on the devil.

Certainly, demonic powers can operate within any economic system, but the only way they're able to do that is through those that work with in that system - actual people. For example, if the individuals working within a monetary system are wicked and evil, then that system can become corrupt. But again that is based on the hearts of people and not the money itself.

People have financial problems because they have a mindset of poverty and lack. This mindset is caused by a lack of teaching, training and education in the arena of finances. Ignorance is not bliss. If one is ignorant on how to utilize the money they have, the end result will be financial instability. Other financial problems are tied to other demonic habits. For example, a person that is bound to drugs, alcohol or a lifestyle of partying will spend their hard earned money in areas that are simply imprudent. This cannot be blamed on demons but it is a matter of ones will and mind being renewed in the area of finances.

Lastly, we see in the story of the unjust steward that he was not an investor. This holds true for many 21st-century believers today. On average, most are not financially literate and do not invest in the numerous financial instruments that are available today. This is unfortunate considering that the Bible tells us as Kingdom citizens to leave an inheritance for our grandchildren. Additionally, the Bible says that we should lend and not borrow. Have you ever considered how you will be able to lend money to others if you yourself do not have any significant money to lend? Financial education among believers is critically important. Actively empowering oneself in this area will not only bless you, but also help advance the Kingdom of God within every sector of society.

Misconception – "Demons come out by Fasting"

This is a common teaching by many. But again, one scripture does not warrant a clearly defined method for casting out demons.

Some people fast to get victory over Satan or demons. However that is unscriptural. The Word of God promises that if we resist Satan, then he will flee from us.

"Therefore submit to God. Resist the devil and he will flee from you." – James 4:7

"Be sober, be vigilant; because your adversary the devil walks about like a roaring lion, seeking whom he may devour. Resist him, steadfast in the faith, knowing that the same sufferings are experienced by your brotherhood in the world." – I Peter 5:8-9

We believe that many people have taken what Jesus spoke about in Matthew chapter 17 completely out of context. Let's take a look.

"Then came the disciples to Jesus apart, and said, Why could not we cast him out? And Jesus said unto them, Because of your unbelief: for verily I say unto you, If ye have faith as a grain of mustard seed, ye shall say unto this mountain, Remove hence to yonder place; and it shall remove; and nothing shall be impossible unto you. Howbeit this kind goeth not out but by prayer and fasting." - Matthew 17:19-21,

In this scenario, the disciples of the Lord came across a man that needed his son to be free from demons. As we see in the scriptures, this demon had his son severely demonized.

"…... for he is an epileptic and suffers severely; for he often falls into the fire and often into the water." - Matthew 17:15

Keep in mind that this statement was only in reference to *one* kind of demon.

Although Jesus' disciples failed to cast out one particular kind of demon, they successfully cast out many other demons.

Most likely, Jesus' disciples were frightened or thought, (based on their fleshly senses,) that they were not capable of contending with this level of demon.

Clearly they struggled with unbelief. Jesus says in verse seventeen:

"O faithless and perverse generation, how long shall I be with you?

Again in verse twenty, Jesus said to them,

"Because of your unbelief; for assuredly, I say to you, if you have faith as a mustard seed, you will say to this mountain, 'Move from here to there,' and it will move; and nothing will be impossible for you. However, this kind does not go out except by prayer and fasting."

The context of the text is focused on the disciple's unbelief, not the demon in the man's son. They had the authority to cast out the demon, but did not believe they could do it. The problem was in them, not the demon in the boy. Unbelief is a demon and clearly the disciples needed to address the unbelief in them.

If Jesus gives someone authority over demons, as He did His twelve disciples, then they have that authority and fasting can't increase it. Fasting does deal with one's flesh and as such, will elevate their spiritual sensitivity and address the doubt they have in their God-given authority.

In Mark's account of the same incident, Jesus is recorded as saying, "This kind cannot come out by anything but prayer" [Mark 9:29]. Interestingly, in the margin of the New American Standard Bible, it's noted that many manuscripts add *"and fasting"* to the end of the verse.

While every believer should live a "fasted" lifestyle, Fasting is not necessary to cast out demons.

Misconception – "Demons are stupid"

This is certainly not true. Demons are part of a highly intelligent network. They're capable of planning, strategizing, remembering and communicating very effectively. Their demonic network of complex lies, skillful deception and profound perversion is clear evidence of their intelligence. Demons are not stupid and must not be taken lightly.

Misconception – "Demons tell the Truth"

I've heard some people say that demons will tell you the truth. No they will not! They will pervert the truth. Demons cannot tell the truth, simply because they are not on the side of truth.

In John 8:44 Jesus said; *"Ye are of your father the devil, and the lusts of your father ye will do. He was a murderer from the beginning, and abode not in the truth, because there is no truth in him. When he speaketh a lie, he speaketh of his own: for he is a liar, and the father of* it."

Clearly, Satan and his demonic host only speak lies.

Misconception – "You must know the names of Demons for them to come out"

While there are many books about demon names there is no express scriptural evidence that warrants having a conversation with demons or inquiring as to what their names are. Much of the support that people give for knowing the names of demons is found in the book of Luke.

In Luke 8:28-33 we find <u>one</u> example of asking a man that was bound by demons "What is your name." In that example, Jesus told the unclean spirit to go out prior to asking the name. This was Jesus first command. Jesus then asked the question, "What is your name?" This represents Jesus second command. Clearly Jesus discerned that there was an entire network in operation in the man's life.

An experienced deliverance minister should be able to spiritually discern and be train in what the characteristics of demons are, but it is not necessary. Throughout the bible Jesus liberated many without asking that question.

Rather than knowing what demon names are, Kingdom believers need to be more concerned with, do the demons know you and the authority you have in Him.

And the evil spirit answered and said, "Jesus I know, and Paul I know; but who are you?" – Acts 19:15

Misconception "A demonic manifestation is the sign of a successful deliverance"

Demons do manifest, but this does not mean they've come out. Demons manifesting is a sign that they're being agitated. However, this can be deceiving and dangerous to the inexperienced deliverance minister to rely on manifestations as a sign of a successful deliverance. It's often a good sign to run into a manifestation during deliverance, but it doesn't necessarily mark a successful deliverance. A successful deliverance will provide genuine and lasting relief for the host. To manifest, means to make known. This has nothing to do with being set free from demons.

Misconception – "You should pray for the sick - only"

The current religious mindset of bringing the sick before the Lord in prayer or praying at a distance for them is not a model that is consistent with the ministry of healing and deliverance as Jesus demonstrated. Jesus taught about the Kingdom of God and then demonstrated that Kingdom by going to the sick and healing them. He then told his disciples to *"go and heal the sick"*, not pray for them from afar. Believers must understand, to the *'nth'* degree that they have the authority to appropriate healing into the lives of those that are sick. While there certainly is nothing wrong with praying for those that are sick, God's will is that you go to them and heal them.

"Other Common Misconceptions"

"You can cast calories out of food" – FALSE

"You can Love demons out of people" - FALSE

"Demon's will attack you if you go into a secular, worldly or evil place" – FALSE

"You can declare and decree demons out of people or entire regions" – FALSE

"You have to be baptized in the Holy Spirit to cast out demons" – FALSE

"You should converse with Demons" – FALSE

"Demons come out by TEXT messages" – FALSE

"Demons come out by Gossip music." - FALSE

"Demons come out by 'pleading the blood" – FALSE

"Believers can't have demon(s)" – FALSE

"You can cast a curse out" - FALSE

"Demons do not cause sickness and disease – FALSE

"Demons come out at the church Altar" – FALSE

"Demons come out by yelling at them" – FALSE

"Demons come out by crying" – FALSE

"Demons come out through the use of artifacts" – FALSE

"Demons come out by oil or Holy Water" – FALSE

"Demons come out by speaking in tongues" – FALSE

"You must lay hands on people in order for demons to come out" – FALSE

"Demons come out by hitting the person" – FALSE

"Demons come out by dancing" – FALSE

"Demons come out by running around the church" – FALSE

"Demons can be "worshipped out" - FALSE

"Deliverance is a one-time 5 second experience" – FALSE

"Deliverance ministry is more effective when done by Apostles " – FALSE

Section Notes:

Section Six
Scriptures Affirming our Authority over Satan and Demons

Scriptures Affirming our Authority over Satan and Demons

You are of God, little children, and have overcome them, because He who is in you is greater than he who is in the world. – I John 4:4

Finally, my brethren, be strong in the Lord and in the power of His might. Put on the whole armor of God, that you may be able to stand against the wiles of the devil. For we do not wrestle against flesh and blood, but against principalities, against powers, against the rulers of the darkness of this age, against spiritual hosts of wickedness in the heavenly places. Therefore take up the whole armor of God, that you may be able to withstand in the evil day, and having done all, to stand. Stand therefore, having girded your waist with truth, having put on the breastplate of righteousness, and having shod your feet with the preparation of the gospel of peace; above all, taking the shield of faith with which you will be able to quench all the fiery darts of the wicked one. And take the helmet of salvation, and the sword of the Spirit, which is the word of God; praying always with all prayer and supplication in the Spirit, being watchful to this end with all perseverance and supplication for all the saints – Ephesians 6:10-18

Therefore submit to God. Resist the devil and he will flee from you. Draw near to God and He will draw near to you. Cleanse your hands, you sinners; and purify your hearts, you double-minded. – James 4:7-8

I have given you authority to trample on snakes and scorpions and to overcome all the power of the enemy; nothing will harm you - Luke 10:19

The God of peace will soon crush Satan under your feet. The grace of our Lord Jesus be with you - Romans 16:20

No, in all these things we are more than conquerors through him who loved us. For I am convinced that neither death nor life, neither angels nor demons . . . will be able to separate us from the love of God that is in Christ Jesus our Lord - Romans 8:37-39

And God raised us up with Christ and seated us with him in the heavenly realms in Christ Jesus, - Ephesians 2:6

The reason the Son of God appeared was to destroy the devil's work - 1 John 3:8

Calling the Twelve to him, he sent them out two by two and gave them authority over evil spirits - Mark 6:7

The seventy-two returned with joy and said, "Lord, even the demons submit to us in your name." - Luke 10:17

I will give you the keys of the kingdom of heaven; whatever you bind on earth will be bound in heaven, and whatever you loose on earth will be loosed in heaven - Matthew 16:19

Then Jesus came to them and said, "All authority in heaven and on earth has been given to me. Therefore go. . . ." - Matthew 28:18

I tell you the truth, anyone who has faith in me will do what I have been doing. He will do even greater things than these, because I am going to the Father - John 14:12

"I will not speak much more with you, for the ruler of the world is coming, and he has nothing in me; - John 14:30

"But if I cast out demons by the Spirit of God, then the kingdom of God has come upon you. - Matthew 12:28

"And this woman, a daughter of Abraham as she is, whom Satan has bound for eighteen long years, should she not have been released from this bond on the Sabbath day?" - Luke 13:16

"You know of Jesus of Nazareth, how God anointed Him with the Holy Spirit and with power, and how He went about doing good and healing all who were oppressed by the devil, for God was with Him. - Acts 10:38

The one who practices sin is of the devil; for the devil has sinned from the beginning The Son of God appeared for this purpose, to destroy the works of the devil. - 1 John 3:8

Therefore, since the children share in flesh and blood, He Himself likewise also partook of the same, that through death He might render powerless him who had the power of death, that is, the devil, and might free those who through fear of death were subject to slavery all their lives. - Hebrews 2:14-15

For He rescued us from the domain of darkness, and transferred us to the kingdom of His beloved Son, - Colossians 1:13

Who gave Himself for us to redeem us from every lawless deed, and to purify for Himself a people for His own possession, zealous for good deeds - Titus 2:14

'He who overcomes, I will grant to him to sit down with Me on My throne, as I also overcame and sat down with My Father on His throne. - Revelation 3:21

"Now judgment is upon this world; now the ruler of this world will be cast out - John 12:31

"Then He will also say to those on His left, 'Depart from Me, accursed ones, into the eternal fire which has been prepared for the devil and his angels - Matthew 25:41

And He said to them, "I was watching Satan fall from heaven like lightning - Luke 10:18

And concerning judgment, because the ruler of this world has been judged - John 16:11

When He had disarmed the rulers and authorities, He made a public display of them, having triumphed over them through Him - Colossians 2:15

For I am convinced that neither death, nor life, nor angels, nor principalities, nor things present, nor things to come, nor powers, nor height, nor depth, nor any other created thing, will be able to separate us from the love of God, which is in Christ Jesus our Lord Romans 8:38-39

And they overcame him because of the blood of the Lamb and because of the word of their testimony, and they did not love their life even when faced with death - Revelation 12:11

They took his advice; and after calling the apostles in, they flogged them and ordered them not to speak in the name of Jesus, and then released them. So they went on their way from the presence of the Council, rejoicing that they had been considered worthy to suffer shame for His name. And every day, in the temple and from house to house, they kept right on teaching and preaching Jesus as the Christ - Acts 5:40-42

I am writing to you, fathers, because you know Him who has been from the beginning I am writing to you, young men, because you have overcome the evil one I have written to you, children, because you know the Father. I have written to you, fathers, because you know Him who has been from the beginning I have written to you, young men, because you are strong, and the word of God abides in you, and you have overcome the evil one -1 John 2:13-14

The God of peace will soon crush Satan under your feet The grace of our Lord Jesus be with you - Romans 16:20

These will wage war against the Lamb, and the Lamb will overcome them, because He is Lord of lords and King of kings, and those who are with Him are the called and chosen and faithful - Revelation 17:14

Then I saw an angel coming down from heaven, holding the key of the abyss and a great chain in his hand. And he laid hold of the dragon, the serpent of old, who is the devil and Satan, and bound him for a thousand years; and he threw him into the abyss, and shut it and sealed it over him, so that he would not deceive the nations any longer, until the thousand years were completed; after these things he must be released for a short time - Revelation 20:1-3

And the sea gave up the dead which were in it, and death and Hades gave up the dead which were in them; and they were judged, every one of them according to their deeds. Then death and Hades were thrown into the lake of fire This is the second death, the lake of fire - Revelation 20:13-14

Other Books by Apostle Robert & Dixie Summers

Deliverance Training Manual - 101©

It's about Time

Genuine Fathers – Willing Sons ©

Kingdom Principles of Success, Wealth & Prosperity ©

Harboring the Spirit of Jezebel ©

Gossip – The Weapon of Mass Destruction ©

Throw Jezebel Down ©

Jezebels Whoredoms, Perversions and Witchcrafts ©

Made in the USA
Middletown, DE
28 August 2017